Real Gusto Comes Later:
How Professional Women Experience
Retirement

Freddie Groomes-McLendon

Editor

SokheChapke Publishing

Published by:
SokheChapke Publishing, Inc., ©
P.O Box 21161
Tallahassee, FL 32316
545 East Tennessee St., Suite 200-A
Tallahassee, FL 32308
Telephone: 866-711-5984
Email: info@sokhechapkepublishing.com
Website: sokhechapkepublishing.com.

ISBN 9780983399193

Library of Congress Card Catalog Data
Groomes-McLendon, Freddie   L.

Published and printed in the United States of America

Table of Contents

Foreword

Jill Quadagno

The transition from work to retirement can transform an individual's social world, relationships and daily routines. There have been numerous studies on the factors that influence how people adjust to retirement. On the positive side, retirees have more freedom and independence than they may have had since they were teenagers. Yet they may also miss a more structured existence and feel the loss of status that accompanies a job. How people feel about their jobs also affects how they feel about leaving those jobs. Professionals who receive intrinsic rewards from work often delay retirement while people who work at routine, unchallenging jobs are often eager to retire. Not surprisingly, happiness in retirement is associated with good health.

The accepted wisdom is that most people decide to retire because of a desire to trade work for leisure. The extremely remarkable women who contributed to this volume contradict much of the accepted wisdom about retirement. All are professional women, highly successful in their chosen fields. Some retired voluntarily while others reached the time limit of the state of Florida's retirement plan. Some have taken the skills they used on their jobs and used them to engage in new activities, often as volunteers. Others have reinvented themselves, embarking on entirely new vocations, whether it be travel, music or returning to school. Although the lives of these women differ in many ways, there are also common themes reflected in all their biographies.

Social Engagement

Many studies have found that retirees who engage in productive activities and maintain strong social networks have a positive sense of well-being and are less likely to be depressed. Alyce Gay Goff provides an excellent illustration of that idea. She is actively engaged in numerous activities, often focused around lifelong passion for music. Music has provided many opportunities for Alice to remain very busy with concerts, choirs, and other performances. Lucy Ho is another example of a retiree who has remained energetically engaged. After "retiring," she opened two restaurants! Lucy is also involved in numerous community organizations. Joel Dawson, a self-described risk-taker, has used the time she now has as a retiree to pursue her love of travel, taking trips to India, Africa and Peru to name just a few places on her exciting and ambitious itinerary. Clinita Ford is another traveler, an octogenarian and adventurer who scorns organized tours and saves her money to take a trip somewhere interesting every year. For Fancy Funk retirement has meant staying involved with people and in various social and civic associations.

Activities cannot just fill time, however, but must be meaningful. Marie Cowart found her days were full following retirement but felt she was too focused on the "busy ethnic." So she reviewed her activities to get more balance and achieve a sense of purpose and quality in relationships. Learning to say no has also been a challenge for Marjorie Turnbull and Freddie Groomes-McLendon, who both have sought to focus on those activities that are meaningful to them and useful for others.

Volunteering

Since the 1970s Americans as a whole have spent less time volunteering in their communities. The exception is people aged 60 and older. In the past quarter century, volunteer work among this group has nearly doubled. What accounts for this rise in volunteer work among older people? Several factors are responsible. Older people are in better health, more highly education and more financially secure than any previous generation. They enjoy longer and more active post-retirement lives than their predecessors.

Volunteering not only helps the people who receive the services provided by the volunteers, it also helps the volunteers themselves. Volunteers gain social approval from others, which in turn improves their self-esteem. Some engage in volunteer activities that take their lives in entirely new directions, while others use the skills they had from their working years to give freely of their time to help others. The contributors to this volume all make enormous contributions to their communities through their volunteer work. Barbara Barnes built on her years of experience in higher education to establish an educational consulting company. Marjorie Turnbull volunteers on the boards of organizations where her experience as a foundation director and fundraising knowledge has been useful. Charlotte Maguire, a physician retired from active practice, continues to use her medical knowledge in a volunteer capacity. Fancy Funk has continued her involvement with fundraising since her retirement.

Family and Friends

Declining mortality has obviously created an unprecedented potential for people at all stages of the life course to be involved in a complex network of kinship relationships and family ties. Retirees today are likely to have living parents and siblings, and although women still outlive men on average, older women today are more likely to have a surviving husband. Many retirees live long enough to see their grandchildren become adults. Being a grandparent is not only an important and enjoyable role but can also be beneficial for the grandchildren. Grandparents help shape the values, identities and beliefs of their grandchildren. Charlotte Maquire's grandfather played an important role in her life, helping her to pursue a career in medicine. Lucy Ho serves as a role model for her grandchildren, telling them to look for new challenges and try new endeavors.

Many women in this volume report on the importance of family in their lives. Joel Dawson shares her love of travel with her husband but also enjoys entertaining family and friends at home. Ruth Hobbs refers to her "awesome mate of 39 plus years." Barbara Barnes explains how her "gusto" really soars when she imagines ways she can involve her husband, family and friends in her unfinished projects. Linda Fulmore explains how she inherited her strong work ethic from her parents. Yet family engagement can also bring increased responsibility. Both before and after retirement, Marie

Cowart cared for a series of relatives, first her aunt and uncle and then her mother-in-law.

Reinventing Oneself

Life expectancy has been rising for more than a century but most people would agree that what matters more than length of life is quality of life. The term that reflects that idea is called "active life expectancy" and the women in this book provide a vivid illustration of this concept. Many have taken the opportunity provided by retirement to tackle new challenges and pursue new paths. At the age of 54 Linda Fulmore took an early retirement package and went back to school to earn a Ph.D. After Penny Ralston left her position as Dean of Human Sciences, she established a center to improve the health and life of underserved populations. Ruth Hobbs is pursuing her deferred dream of acting and modeling.

Spirituality

Religion can provide comfort and social support in later life. Numerous studies have found a positive association between religion and well-being and various measures of physical health. People express their faith in various ways from public activities like attending services to private activities such as praying. Although attendance at services is a commonly-used measure of religiosity, the non-organizational features of religion – faith and spirituality – are equally important.

Ruth Hobbs mentions the importance of her spiritual life which guides her treatment of other people. Alyce Goff believes that she must use what she has for God's glory. Freddie Groomes-McLendon's faith in God helped her survive a divorce on the eve of her retirement and the deaths of her mother and son. Penny Ralston also speaks of her strong faith and her belief that she was put on earth for a reason. All these women in various ways are deeply spiritual.

People who fear aging need look no further than this book to find a source of inspiration. All these women have led productive careers and now in retirement, each in her own unique way has found satisfaction and fulfillment. As Clinita Ford says, "how sweet it is."

Introduction

Freddie L. Groomes-McLendon

"Over the hill", "Has Beens", "Out of Touch", "Antiques" , "Slow Pokes", "Ole School" and the descriptions go on when it comes to describing retirees. This may be a result of the definition contained in Webster "Retired- withdrawn, secluded, withdrawn from business or public life, to remove from active service". How out dated are these definitions? Others believe that retirees are the recipient s of a well- deserved break after years of hard work and service. Most retirees, I believe are mentally sharp, flexible and sometimes fancy free and active in a myriad of activities and continue to make real contributions to society and their families.

Retirees and the 65 and older set are obviously the fastest growing population in America. Unfortunately, the old definition may apply to some, but I believe it is a small minority.

A better definition I believe is that retirees are an experienced and capable group of individuals with valuable expertise and wisdom that can be made available where needed at little or no cost. They still have to varying degrees, enthusiasm and commitment to service and building a better society.

Having retired about six years ago following

forty-five years of active service in Higher Education, life for me currently is wonderful. I am active and involved, but only in those things that I chose to be involved in and that please me. Curiosity motivated me to inquire of some of my colleagues to determine just how they were fairing. Well, I'm please to say that most were enjoying retirement as I. Unfortunately there were some who felt guilty about retirement, were bored, felt that they didn't prepare adequately financially and had to return to gainful employment and still others felt lost and disconnected. This realization left me perplexed because, I sincerely believe that "Real Gusto Comes Later" or at least it should. Retirees deserve real gusto after many years of significant and excellent service.

I decided to call some of my productive retired friends and colleagues and share my concern. It generated so much interest and enthusiasm that I came up with the idea of writing a collaborative book.

I asked some of those retirees who were willing to address the concerns that had been raised by offering alternatives on how they have found purpose, satisfaction, pleasure and the ability to contribute to society during retirement. Yielding what I chose to label "Real Gusto Comes Later."

Gusto is sometimes defined as "vigorous enjoyment, fondness, taste, liking." Think about it. If properly planned, in retirement you can become the center of your day's activity. You schedule what you want, when you want, and with whom you want, if you want to. You can sleep in or get up at your leisure. You can select those who you care to interact with and avoid others unlike the situation in employment. You can travel domestically or internationally or choose not to travel at all. You can see and do things that you use to dream of and take your time in doing it. Retirement can be blissful.

In a recent public radio broadcast Jane Pauley made an awakening comment. She said women are now expected to live 40 years beyond the initial life expectancy for women. Wow, why not strive for a good quality of life laced with gusto.

In the following chapters you will read of the experiences of several of my friends and colleagues that I think have indeed found gusto later. Their perspectives are unique to them but have the potential of sparking your interest and even stimulating you to do something similar.

If you are an educator, relative, friend or care giver of a retiree you should benefit from the experiences of these writers. If you are in fact a member of this select class of citizens, a retiree, you may after reading some of the chapters be stimulated to try and do something that has been gnawing at you for some time but you just couldn't find the "moving desire" for action.

The writers represent a diverse group of professional women ranging in age up to their mid-nineties. Their noteworthy professions include medicine, education, entrepreneurs, politicians, administrators, musicians, artist, care givers and the list goes on. Hopefully, you will be able to relate personally to one or more of these writers and be stimulated to discover GUSTO LATER!

Achieving Real Gusto Through Exploring New Adventures

Ruth Hobbs

In reflection, the anonymous quote, "Youth is wasted on the young", has proven to be a truism in my life. Most often, young people have everything going for them. Physically, they're in the best health they will ever be in; their minds are sharp and clear, but they lack patience, understanding and wisdom which resulted in so much wasted effort. I have found that "Real Gusto" of life or the vigorous and enthusiastic enjoyment of life really does come later.

It comes when wisdom meets with patience and the understanding that life is really a continual journey based on the attitudes that are formed early in life.

It comes when one has acquired the patience, understanding and wisdom that tell you not to "sweat the small things" and the realization that most of the situations you face in life are really, in the cosmic order, "small things". I agree with one of the few true televangelist of this age, Chuck Swindoll, who wrote, "I am convinced that life is ten percent what happens to me and ninety percent how I react to it. And so it is with you. We are in charge of our attitudes."

Taking charge of our attitude is no easy feat. We all grow up wanting the best career, wanting that perfect mate, and yes, wanting that care-free but successful life. The problem is, life is full of bumps and turns. I suggest that success in life depends on how well you navigate those turns and handle those bumps. Being in charge of your attitude, I have found, is the key.

While it is no easy feat, taking charge of your attitude is most often the product of a life-long commitment to learning from those who have had a measure of success in their lives. For me, the core learning came from my mother and grandmother. Their teaching and guidance shaped my attitudes and influenced the actions I have taken in life. My mother and grandmother had sayings that became indelibly etched in my mind. I internalized them as guiding principles for my life. Little did I know that these nuggets of wisdom would help me avoid the wasted efforts that are common to youthful hubris. These sayings have and continue to allow me the patience, understanding and wisdom which are now part and parcel of who I am as a mature adult. They have been incorporated in every aspect of my life; personal, academic, professional, and more. In fact, even in my retirement, I can still hear the sayings of my mother and grandmother:

"Hard work never killed anybody"

"Find strength in purpose"

"Anything worth doing is worth doing well"

"You get as good as you give"

"If you are powerful, you must be merciful"

Taken as principles for living, these statements have allowed me to have a successful and rewarding family life, career and deeper spiritual life.

I have realized time and time again that working hard at what I wanted to accomplish always resulted I my receiving more than I could have ever imagined. At a very young age, throughout elementary and high school years, I put forth all the effort I could muster and thought necessary to accomplish what I set out to do. It was always hard work but "Hard work never killed anybody". In fact, every time I did this I was rewarded with important accomplishments such as: winning quite a few school-wide contests, receiving prestigious awards/scholarships for academic accomplishments, being chosen for school/district leadership roles. Later, throughout college and during my young adult years hard work resulted in receiving undergraduate and graduate degrees, both with honors; getting married and starting a journey with my life-long partner; starting a family, having two adorable and bright children and one awesome step-child; beginning a career which would eventually lead to a successful professional life.

Working hard and heeding my mother's words that "hard work never killed anybody" gave me cause to put forth the effort in whatever I pursued. If I wanted a healthy loving, stable, God-centered environment in which my relationship with my husband and my children would grow and flourish, then I had to work hard for it. I did. If I wanted all the materialistic nuances and niceties (house, cars, clothes, jewelry, vacations, club memberships, etc.), then I knew I had to work hard for them. I did. If I wanted a successful career and be able to climb that professional ladder to the top, then I knew I had to work hard for it. I did. If I wanted to be able to retire and enjoy all the things that I was too busy to truly enjoy before, then I knew I had to work hard for it. I did. And now, I have that spiritual peace, that awesome mate of 39 plus years, great children and grandchildren, that house on a hill, that terminal degree, financial security, and all of the things necessary to living life with "gusto". I'm having a ball enjoying every moment. Of course, now I'm working hard at having fun!

While not being hesitant to work hard to accomplish what I wanted was a good thing, I found that working hard without a clear purpose is just hard work. I had to couple the "Hard work never killed anybody" saying with one that told me to "Find strength in purpose." This was never more needed than when I went through the grueling period of working to finish my terminal degree. I was a mate, a mother, an employee and all while working to endure the rigors that come with working toward a terminal degree. I cannot say that there was never a time that giving up did not cross my mind. It did and I had to find the strength to continue in defining my purpose.

The purpose was to do all that I could do to be academically prepared to make a difference in my profession. While having a PhD, alone, the highest degree in my field, does not totally prepare a person for a career in education, the pursuit and acquiring it is an indicator that one is serious about that chosen profession.

Further, I reasoned that the sayings of my mother and grandmother made it clear that if I were to be an educator, one who impacted the lives of those who would be our future leaders, I should heed the words "Anything worth doing is worth doing well." This attitude carried me successfully through a 35 year career that began as a grade school teacher, then an assistant principal, then principal and ending as a school district-level administrator. At each level, I was constantly inwardly challenged by the admonition that "Anything worth doing is worth doing well."

Lest it appears that my professional career was a straight road paved with success, let me add that it was not. I had my share of bumps and turns in the road. Whether the turns or bumps were fueled by professional jealousy, success envy or even political treachery, I chose to face each one with the invaluable principles taught me and the aforementioned words of Chuck Swindoll, "I am convinced that life is ten percent what happens to me and ninety percent how I react to it. And so it is with you. We are in charge of our attitudes."

Another attitude that has proven true to me and has been a large part of the success I have enjoyed in life is the admonition from my mother and grandmother that in life "You get as good as you give."

Too often we succumb to the tendency to put our lives on cruise control. This is the reason that many get up each morning complaining" Oh God! Another day?" When you take the attitude that in life "You get as good as you give", you approach each new day of life joyfully and thankfully declaring "Thank God! Another day!" For me, each day of life is a new day to savor and approach with "gusto."

Any measure of success will bring with it the ability to influence another's life. That is called power. Whether it is a teacher or manager or officer in some organization, any measure of success will bring with it a sense or realization of power. I have found that it has always served me well to remember that "If you are powerful, you must be merciful".

While I learned this from my mother and grandmother, I also found it to be a Biblical requirement. There is no power but that which is granted from above. We are called to walk humbly with our God, do justice and love mercy. This is the core of my spiritual life and the template on how I treat everyone that I interact with. Whether professionally, casually or on a personal level, I have found that life flows smoother when you realize that any success and power derived from it has the requirement that says "If you are powerful, you must be merciful".

To all of my sisters who would seek a meaningful and purposeful life, I offer these words on my life experiences as both encouragement and advice.

I am now at the point that I can reflect on this life journey and say that while you should always go for the gusto it's the real gusto that comes later in life. It comes when you can say goodbye to the tension and hello to the pension.

I recently retired and I am having the most fabulous time of my life. I decided to reinvent myself and to delve into an area outside of my educational "comfort zone". In pursuit of that deferred dream, I decided to explore acting and modeling and I'm doing so with a great deal of gusto! Although I am new to the "business" and have a lot to learn, I am enjoying every moment. Thus far I have read parts and auditioned for a few small roles in plays and television. I have been photo selected as an extra for commercial work as well as for a television series. Recently, I modeled (along with my husband) for an advertisement in a children's magazine…. now that was fun! Even more recently I participated in my first professional fashion show. Although I was somewhat nervous, I must say walking that runway was exciting and exhilarating. As I prepare for my next fashion show which will be at my sorority's national convention, I will focus on making sure I am physically and mentally ready for the challenge. Well, I suppose that eating right and exercise will be the order of things. Anything worth doing…; "Hard work…; "Find strength…: "You get as good…: Anyway, you get the message.

Just as the advice of my mother and grand-mother rang true to my ears helping to guide me through life, so too did the words of a former col-league. Upon her retirement she shared the idea that you should plan as much for your retirement as you did for your career.

Those words resonated in my mind the mo-ment I knew it was time to move on to another phase of my life…retirement. Immediately, I start-ed planning for what that might look like. Self-reinvention, rejuvenation, and fulfillment were all paramount toward realizing a meaningful retire-ment. I envisioned retirement as the time to finally do some of those things that I dreamed of doing but never had the time to do.

I embraced the idea of self-reinvention by getting involved in activities totally unrelated to my career life. I am living my dream of becoming an actor and a model. Taking classes, studying scripts, traveling and networking with others, in preparation for my newly found self, has been rejuvenating and fulfilling.

Self-reinvention, rejuvenation and fulfillment are definitely not limited to spending time realizing my dream deferred. I am reconnecting with and enjoying each day with my spouse of 39+ years. We put forth just as much gusto in the ordinary things as well as the extraordinary things that we do together. Visiting our favorite stores; going to the health club; traveling and exploring new places; meeting new people; rekindling old friendships; devoting time to our favorite charities; participating in church and community activities; or just sitting on the patio enjoying the pleasure of each other's company. In short, we are unwinding and savoring all the gusto-filled moments that we were too busy raising a family and being involved in our careers before to enjoy.

The real gusto for me at this stage of my life is also evidenced through my role as grandma to two lovable, yet very active grandchildren. Being able to spend time with them and to get involved in various activities with them brings a great deal of pleasure to my life. High energy and gusto are definitely appropriate terms to use when it comes to my "grands". They bring a whole new meaning to the idea of high level of energy, enthusiasm and real gusto which convinces me that retirement does not mean being tired!

To borrow a saying from my husband, "If anybody had told me that retirement was this much fun, I would never have gone to work." At this point, all I can say is WOW! Needless-to-say, I am having THE most fabulous time of my life and doing so with lots of GUSTO.

At every level of your life, go for the GUSTO but do it with the understanding that you may have to defer dreams and make difficult sacrifices. Just know, however, that when it is all said and done, your attitudes and the people you allow to shape those attitudes will determine where you end up.

Reinventing Yourself

Penny A. Ralston

I have reinvented myself. In the past four years, I have moved from serving as a dean of human sciences at a major research university to being involved in community health with a focus on health equity. Most of my time is spent either working with community organizations to improve health or mentoring students for the health professions. But the reinvention is not something totally new. It evolved from interests and learning developed over a lifetime. Although I am not retired, this reinvention is a transition to a new life with many of the same challenges and opportunities one finds in becoming retired. There are dimensions to this transition that are a first glance professional but on further examination deeply personal. How did I come to this point in my life? This chapter outlines my journey.

The Calling

I think I have been called. No, I have not been called into the ministry. But I have a purpose in life that becomes clearer every day. It is a calling to help people. Very simple, yet complex in how it is manifested. I am deeply spiritual, perhaps more than one might imagine in knowing me. I am not one who is demonstrative or even very verbal about it. But my very being is connected to strong faith. I believe that I was put on this earth for a reason and that the broader plan is being revealed. Various events in my life only confirm these beliefs, including being a resilient child during various chal- lenges in my youth, being provided with numerous mentors who helped to guide my life, and meeting and marrying the love of my life, Chester Davis, a native Hoosier who I met in Massachusetts. This spiritual context provides the backdrop for my jour- ney, from the early years, through professional de- velopment and the new venture.

The Early Years

In reflecting back, I realized that this reinven- tion had its roots early in my life. I grew up on a 215-acre farm in Indiana that my parents bought in 1949. Both were first generation African-Americans from Richmond, Indiana. They moved to a rural ar- ea near Modoc, Indiana, a predominantly White community that historically had included people of African descent. Cabin Creek, a Black rural com- munity was to the North of Modoc, settled by freed slaves from Virginia and North Carolina. The Un- derground Railroad was active during slavery in this area. Growing up in this kind of "Black community" was unique. My family attended Modoc Bethel Afri- can Methodist Episcopal Church with the remnants of the families from Cabin Creek since most of the families had moved away by this time. We went to school with other Black children from Losantville—a small town near Modoc--who were, like us, the late arrivers to Cabin Creek. My father purchased the farm on contract, taking the risk of losing the property if a payment was missed. My mother worked the farm along with my father and ran the household. We were, for the most part, self-contained. We produced our own milk and eggs, had three gardens and froze or canned for the winter, and butchered chickens, hogs and cattle for meat. My mother also made all of our clothes.

Life was not easy for a variety of reasons. Perhaps the biggest challenge we faced was my father's health. A diabetic, my father suffered from many of the complications of the disease including amputation of both legs, and eventually glaucoma that left him almost totally blind before he died. Most of my childhood memories were of my family trying to maintain his health, treatment in hospitals, recovery at home and then the cycle starting all over again. Amazingly, during recovery he would be back outside farming once again, even with prostheses on his legs. My mother learned the farm business the best she could and would eventually take over decision-making as my father's health worsened.

I learned much from these early years that inform the present. The sense of vision my parents must have had to take this farm with all it did not have—old, frame house with no running water, no indoor bathroom—and see the possibilities. The backbreaking work that it took to make ends meet and to ensure that basic needs were met. The stress they must have faced when the crops failed to come in as planned or when a hog died unexpectedly--stress that led to internal strife that took a toll on their marriage. The racism they no doubt experienced when they could not get a loan. Or, when the contract was "called in" when a payment was missed. Parenthetically, my father stood tall that day with rifle on his lap, ready to meet the man if he happened by with the news that we would have to move. What I realized was that my parents took risks to make a life for their children. Possibly no different than other African-Americans or other people in general whose lives might have been much harsher. But to me, these two people overcame many challenges and saw opportunity in the lives of their children.

With the challenges we faced as a family, school life became an oasis of sort. There were three daughters and I was the youngest. My oldest sister had a different father and was with us briefly but then moved to live with her biological father. My middle sister and I both attended the local pre-dominantly White school. We were both good students and found the teachers welcoming and supportive. I was encouraged to take college prep courses and did well in them, graduating as salutatorian. I enjoyed organizations and was a member of 4-H and Girl Scouts. I found in these organizations a way to achieve and also found a sense of community that I needed as I was growing and maturing. Organizational leadership was natural for me, not necessarily because I was good at it but because I was likeable and ended up getting elected. I will never forget my first Presidency. I was elected as President of my 4-H Club. I had no preparation so I know it was just a popularity contest but after winning I did the best I could to try to lead. This happened again when I was elected President of the National Honor Society and Cheer-Block Captain. After a while I realized that others saw me as a leader and I worked through my anxieties to develop my leadership skills. Even with the anxieties, I loved school and community organizations and achieving in both.

Professional Development

My professional life included teaching at various levels, from middle school through doctoral level students. I moved from Marion, Indiana where I had my first teaching position following receiving the bachelor's degree from Ball State University to the University of Illinois at Champaign-Urbana where I received the doctorate. I then accepted a teaching position at Iowa State University and there honed my administrative skills, first finding chairing committees interesting work and then moving on to serving as an intern assistant dean of the graduate college. After nine years, I left Iowa State and accepted a position as department chair of home economics at the University of Massachusetts. After five tumultuous years in the late 1980's/early 1990's in a highly political state going through the economic decline of the time, I left Massachusetts for the deanship at Florida State University. I left behind a department that had revamped its curriculum and had a new name (consumer studies). I also became aware of my ability to work toward a shared vision, and at a more basic level, became politically savvy, both inside and outside the academy. Massachusetts was a precursor for Florida State where I moved into an even more political environment. Again the experience was good. I served as dean of human sciences for 14 years. During that time, enrollment more than tripled, faculty received 35 awards for teaching and research and generated close to $2M in new contract and grant awards annually, $18M was raised in two capital campaigns, and a $5.3M building renovation was completed.

Home economics was my main discipline from undergraduate through doctoral level; I never specialized in any one area because I loved the flexibility that being a generalist provided. Social studies, which was my second major in undergraduate school (and my favorite subject in high school), helped me to frame my interest in individual, family and community well-being within a broader societal context. Gerontology was my specialty in my doctoral program because I became interested in the welfare of individuals and families as they age and how the community could provide support for and services to them. What home economics also allowed me to do was to work across disciplines quite easily which led to many opportunities to collaborate on projects.

Throughout my professional life, I found certain "areas of learning" that led to skill sets important then as well as now. These included leadership, collaborations and outreach. As an extension of my earlier years, leadership is one consistent area of learning throughout my life. I found over time that it was a natural process for me to become a leader in various situations, ranging from chairing committees at Iowa State to becoming dean at Florida State. Other leadership opportunities surfaced as well, including holding various elected positions in the American Association of Family and Consumer Sciences, eventually becoming President.

Collaboration and outreach both became increasingly important, first as the normal academic activities of conducting multidisciplinary research and performing public service. What I found, however, was that both of these would lead to a new labor of love. While in Massachusetts, I started working with a nutrition faculty member on a project related to dietary quality and older African Americans. My previous work focused on community based programs for older adults, so this was a related and likely progression.

As a possible result of this work, I received an invitation to write a review of literature for a monograph on health promotion and African American elders. I had not written anything in health at this point. Yet I found the opportunity to review literature on health from a multidisciplinary perspective quite interesting, especially considering the opportunities and challenges in health faced by this population. I hearkened back to my own father's diabetic condition and learned about the disease burden of Blacks as they aged not only for this disease but also for many others such as cardiovascular disease and cancer. Although not recognized at the time, this became an important turning point for my "re-invention." But an even larger turning point was getting ready to happen.

In 1993, I was invited to join The Links, Inc., an African American women's civic organization. Jessie Furlow, M.D., a local physician from Gadsden County, was invited to join the same year and we went through the orientation together. We were required to develop a "project" that could be eventually implemented to help the community. We chose to develop a project that would bring people together once a year for a community health seminar to improve health in the African American community. "Relate, Renew, Re-energize" became a reality between 1999 and 2004, with six highly successful seminars held under the sponsorship of The Links, Inc. This kind of outreach was different from anything I had done previously. In Iowa, I had chaired the Gerontology Workshop Series for seven years and had served on numerous boards while on faculty at all three institutions. Nothing equaled the satisfaction of working with others in the community to address a problem. This was not "performing public service" with the university reaching out to "help others." This was "with the community, for the community." Another turning point was occurring. What became clear to me was that a career that appeared to be heading up the university ladder (yes, I had this vague goal of being a university president some day...) was now going in a different direction. I no longer wanted to move vertically but to use what I had learned in leadership, collaboration and outreach to work in the community.

Establishing a New Venture

By the time I stepped down from being dean of the College of Human Sciences, I knew clearly what I wanted to do in my "post-deaning life" and that was to focus all of my attention on the community with a focus on health. Thus in June 2006, I established the Center on Better Health and Life for Underserved Populations that has the mission of improving the health and life of underserved populations through research and program development. The need for community health is compelling. As a society, the U.S. spends billions on health care annually yet Americans are less healthy than they were a generation ago. In fact, obesity and overweight, a risk factor for several chronic disease conditions such as cardiovascular disease and diabetes, are at epidemic proportions. Until the most recent health reform legislation, 46 million people in

U.S. were without health insurance. And disparities are pervasive across all aspects of health including health status, availability of health professionals and health information, and access to health care. Increasingly, there is a need to translate health information that we already know to the public, especially disparate groups that might have barriers to receiving and using this information.

Establishing the Center was not easy. By this time, I had no mentors to turn to so I had to find the resources I needed myself to make this new venture successful. I learned many lessons in the first two years that may be helpful to others who are transitioning from one phase of life into another:

- Have a passion for the new venture. Obviously, as we get older, time is not on our side. There is no time to waste on "filler" activities or distractions. If you have not done so already, figure out what you love and focus your new venture around it.
- Think big and aspirational. How we spend our time in our latter years obviously will vary by individual interests, but for me having a social purpose is of utmost importance. I want to know that others—not only those I am serving locally—will benefit. So I developed a Center that serves locally but has implications for the state and the nation.
- Plan carefully and practically. Although a broad vision is important, starting a new venture clearly requires attention to details. Similar to starting a business, I had to develop the concept and the action plan, including

a proposed budget. I also knew that I would have to start small.

- <u>Mentor yourself</u>. You may find that there is no one left to mentor you so mentor yourself! Find out what you need, strategize to get the resources, and go for it.
- <u>Take calculated risks.</u> In starting a new venture, sometimes taking risks are important for the overall viability of your project. As an example, I knew that where the Center was located would be important for the clients we would serve. Further, I wanted autonomy in choosing the kind of environment in which to work. So instead of asking the university to find space for the Center, I decided to rent space which had obvious financial consequences but provided independence and lessened the disruption of having to move due to funding issues or campus politics.
- <u>Handle uncertainty</u>. Starting a new venture means that there will be many uncertainties. Will grants be funded? Will students be interested? Would the community welcome our effort? Learning how to manage these uncertainties began with having faith in the project and knowing it is related to my life's purpose.
- <u>Enjoy the process every day</u>. The process of life increasingly becomes important with age because long-term goal setting is not as relevant. If the passion is focused and you have planned appropriately, then the process of building your new venture makes every day special. You are doing what you love...your life's work.

Since the establishment of the new venture, much has happened. In fact, my life has gone in some exciting new directions. The Center received a $1.75 M grant from the National Institutes of Health (NIH) to conduct a five year project on reducing cardiovascular risk in African Americans through church-based health programs. Other smaller grants have been secured as well. I'm now serving on NIH review panels and at the state level serve on the Biomedical Research Advisory Council that is responsible for $40 M in research funds. Also, the Center was involved in the establishment of a statewide organization, the Florida Alliance for Health Professions Diversity.

My reinvention with this new venture is a benefit in a variety of ways. From the community perspective, I am working in a participatory way with leaders and constituents, bringing both information and economic resources to improve health. From the university perspective, I am now collaborating across disciplines to establish and implement projects with faculty and training students in community-based research. From a spiritual perspective, I feel I am fulfilling my purpose to improve the health and life of underserved populations. I feel engaged and stimulated daily as I do this work. I am reinvented.

Achieving Real Gusto Through The Performing Arts

Alyce Gay Goff

I am Alyce Gay Goff, 92 years young. I am a living witness that real gusto comes later in life. It has for me. I achieve real gusto by tickling the ivories almost every day. I've been playing the piano since I was 8 years old, and I have never stopped. Whether you call it a hobby, a passion, or a way of life, my God-given talent has opened doors for me and allowed me to make a difference in this world. It keeps me from ever being bored and restless. There is always something to do. The story of my life may well be divided into four parts: (1) family background; (2) educational background; (3) professional career; and (4) retirement years. For the purpose of this chapter I will concentrate on the retirement years.

As you read my story, I would like for you to think about ...your passion...that hobby you have ...your blessing in your community. In doing so, it will help you will see there are a few <u>KEYS</u> in my success repertoire. It is my goal to help you be able play all the right <u>NOTES</u> in the opus of your successful endeavors. (Pardon the puns.)

I have always made it my business to locate and associate with other people who were active. I discovered that like-minded people are good to associate with. Also please notice that I was not hindered by relocating to a new city. I believe we must use what we have for God's glory no matter where we are. God has given us all gifts. Retirement and age do not diminish that gift. God has been marvelously good to me, and the piano has been "The Wind Beneath My Wings" that God used to move me, mold me and use me for His glory. When I add up all the years (I'm in my 31st), I have done more after retirement than I ever could have during the 37 years that I worked as a public school teacher in the state of Texas. First I was choir director at Jarvis Christian College in Hawkins, TX, and then I taught music in the Abilene, Amarillo and West Independent School District.   When that ended, I said, "not yet." I never wanted to slow down. Retirement just meant that I had more time to do what I really wanted to do, that's all, and you might want to know what I have done with my music and how those activities put real gusto into my life. Since my retirement years have spanned **three decades**, I thought it would be interesting to take you with me down memory lane. Are you ready? Let's go!

In May 1979 after 20 years of service to the West Independent School District (Texas) I retired from public school music teaching. During **The First Decade Of My Retirement (1979-1989)**, I got involved with many activities. Immediately upon retirement I joined the Waco McLennan County Retired Teachers Association. The association stressed to its members the importance of volunteer services. I took this opportunity to work two days a week with the little ones at Laura Edwards Christian Early Learning Center (Waco) teaching music activities to classes of two-year olds through six-years old. I had the grandest time of my life! It was so much fun getting down on the floor with them, playing games and singing fun songs. Most of all, you should have seen me doing the hula-hoop! At 61 years of age! I enjoyed it so much I worked there for a whole year. There's real gusto for you! Also I managed my time so I could sub for music teachers in the Waco ISD. As the saying goes, "You may take the teacher out of the classroom but you can't take the classroom out of the teacher". Yes, that describes me to a 'T'! I enjoyed going to the various campuses, meeting new people and working with students in all areas of the city.

Then in the spring of 1982 my husband died; his death left me devastated, as you can imagine. After a period of about two years, I decided it was time to gradually get on with my life; my husband was gone and the children had "flown the coop" leaving me with an empty nest – I had to do some-thing. Here again, it was music that brought me back to life. I was invited to become a member of the Waco Civic Chorus (1984-1990), Hallelujah! There's nothing like music that will bring you out of the doldrums, as a member, I met others who were into classical music. It was a pleasure to rehearse with them one and a half hour each week (except summers). I looked forward to the performances with the Waco Symphony Orchestra in Waco Hall on the campus of Baylor University. We performed works of the masters such as Bach's <u>Christmas Ora-torio</u>, Handel's <u>Messiah</u>, and Mozart's <u>Requiem</u>, among others. It was thrilling to perform before packed audiences.

My love for music has added gusto to other lives in ways I would never had expected. In 1984 and 1985 I presented Antigone Overstreet, mezzo-soprano, in recital at Wesley UMC in Waco, Texas. In 1986 I presented Glen Beals, tenor, in recital also at Wesley UMC. Their repertoires included works of the masters, secular compositions, hymns and spirituals. Both were young college students with exceptional talent. After attending Glen's recital, the head of the music department at Paul Quinn College (Waco Campus) asked me would I be interested in accompanying the concert choir. Would I? You bet! I spent four very enjoyable years, 1986 - 1990, with those young people, traveling with them, preparing other programs, assisting the director in preparing baccalaureate and commencement music. The last year of my four years was historic. By May of 1990 I had become interim director of the choir; therefore, I was the last director on the Waco campus. Also my daughter was among the last graduates. It made me feel good to know I played for her graduation. I had always looked forward to commencement; I liked the pomp and circumstance of it all. It always gave me a thrill to don academic regalia as well.

Before I leave the first decade, let me tell you about the time I was invited to play for the Waco Chapter of Links, Inc. As I recall the Waco chapter hosted the Western region on a weekend sometime during the latter 80's. This invitation filled me with pride and joy, for them to even think I was good enough to play for such a prestigious organization. After their wine and cheese reception, I played for their black-tie banquet. I also accompanied a jazz singer who was descendant of the famous Mills Brothers Family. The next day I played for their

Sunday morning breakfast and worship service before they departed for home.

I am now entering **The Second Decade Of My Retirement (1990 - 1999)** and "I Don't Feel No-Ways Tired". More than likely, this passion I have for the piano is one of the reasons (in addition to God's grace) that I am still here and in relatively good shape. I have no major health problems.

When it became eminent that Paul Quinn College would be relocating to Dallas, Texas, in the summer of 1990, to occupy the campus left vacant by Bishop College, I was determined that PQ wasn't going to leave me behind! So in August of that same year I stepped out on faith and moved to Dallas as well. Working with the choir had given me real gusto. They say working with students keeps you young. From 1990-1993, I continued as accompanist for the PQ concert choir with Otis J. Lloyd directing. We did more traveling to area conferences of the AME church, more local appearances and more campus activities. More gusto!

They say when you move to a new location, **join, join, join!** The first thing I did was to join church, Camp Wisdom UMC, in the fall of 1990. Soon after, their musician moved back to Fort Worth. Can you guess what happened next? You are right! I was asked to play until they found an organist. It is always good to become a part of a congregation of believers, very friendly people. However, in 1992 I was called to Crest-Moore King UMC and remained there until 2008.

More Joining! In the spring of 1991 I transferred my membership from Waco Alumnae to the Dallas Alumnae Chapter of Delta Sigma Theta Sorority, Inc. and have remained a member to the present year 2010. In 1992 I celebrated 50 years of membership in Delta. As one of the chapter musicians, I took pride in playing for various activities, such as, The Jabberwock, Founders Day Luncheons and Sisterhood Luncheons. Also I sing with the Delta Voices.

Believe it or not, I still found more to do! In the fall of 1992, upon invitation, I joined the South Dallas Concert Choir, a voluntary organization that is a part of the Neighborhood Touring Program sponsored by the City of Dallas office of Cultural affairs. By volunteering my time as a member of this choir, I have the opportunity to give lots of service all over the city. The choir is sent to diverse locations, performing in venues such as recreation centers, senior centers, nursing homes, churches and more. The choir makes some 30 appearances per year. I have been a member for 18 years, and as it stands, I am the oldest member of the group. It is a joy!

Now For An Aha Moment! About 1993 it seemed to me that after all the playing during the first decade, why not have some business/calling cards made and let people know of my passion for playing for social events. So I did. As a result I got quite a few "gigs". I added my son Joseph on bass, his friend on saxophone, and a drummer and vocalist. We formed a combo called **The Evening Breeze**. Our first gig was entertaining at the Delta's Founders Banquet in January of 1995 at the Black Academy of Arts and Letters. Needless to say, I got a big thrill out of it. Our guests seemed to enjoy it also. Imagine me playing with a combo!

In April of 1997 The Delta Dears of Dallas Alumnae Chapter of Delta Sigma Theta Sorority, Inc. presented me and friends in concert at Texas

Discovery Gardens, Fair Park, Dallas. Guest performers included pianists, vocalists, and instrumentalists. We did some classical, secular, show tunes and jazz. It was quite a thrill to perform in this beautiful facility.

In the fall of 1997 in keeping with my intention to join, join, join, upon invitation I joined the Dallas Metroplex Musicians Association (DMMA), which is an affiliate of the National Association of Negro Musicians, Inc., an organization that was established in Chicago in 1919. Becoming a member of this organization really widened my horizon in that I was able to meet and mingle with local musicians as well as those from all over the United States at the national conventions.

Now we are entering *My Third Decade Of Retirement (2000-2010)*. Well, you might ask, "are we there yet?" The answer is "not quite, I have a few more things to tell you". This decade consisted of many memorable performances and award presentations. On occasion and by invitation I was asked to share my music with the community by providing entertainment for various events sponsored by local civic, religious, educational and social organizations.

One such organization was the Curator's Forum of the African American Museum in Fair Park, Dallas, Texas. In the spring of 2000 the Forum initiated a series of events called "Tea @ Three" which met on Thursdays at the museum. I played the tea-room music. At one of these teas I asked Bobby Simmons to sing a song or two. When Dr. Robinson, CEO, heard him sing, he invited us to present a series of recitals in conjunction with his exhibit on the life of Paul Robeson. Immediately following we gave three mini recitals featuring songs that the great singer had made famous such as "Old Man River".

Another invitation came from Dean Hill, director of the Big D band at Townview Magnet High School. In the spring semester of 2000 he asked me to accompany his band students in University Interscholastic League (UIL) competition. I was happy to do so; it was just like old times, working with young people again. My assignment was to work with a trumpet player, trombone player and a clarinet ensemble all of whom were playing class 1 music (more difficult). That meant lot of practice for me, but I loved it. My players advanced to state. I traveled to Austin, TX, on the first weekend in June, on a Friday night with my students so as to be there bright and early for Saturday's competition. The highlight of the trip for me was performing on the stage in the performance hall at the University of Texas and playing on their concert grand! My students earned Division I rating from the judges and I receive compliments for my accompanying. My, oh, my. How good I felt!

Also during this decade I was proud to receive and accept invitations to provide music for Delta Sigma Theta Sorority, Inc., Dallas alumnae Chapter Founders' Day Programs; the National Coalition of 100 Black Women, Inc. Dallas Chapter Annual Scholarship Awards programs and African American Women Bridge Builders' Recognition Luncheon. Also the St. Philip's School and Community Center Diversity Awards Luncheon, Dallas, the Dallas South District Lay Speakers Banquet of The United Methodist Church, and the Irving Texas Black Arts Council's presentation of "an Evening of Gospel Music".

Perhaps one of the most memorable performances of the decade occurred when Crest-Moore King United Methodist Church presented the Goff Family in concert in July of 2007. This was truly a family affair – son, daughter, son-in law, sister-in-law, nieces, and granddaughter. Each exhibited his/her own special talent.

As I stated earlier, "I Don't Feel No-Ways Tired". In the fall of 2008 I was called to serve as musician at Glen Oaks United Methodist Church in Dallas. As soon as I sat down at the piano, they started asking me to present a musical. Our first production was called Command Performances (April 2009). Various choirs, soloists and musicians were sent a scroll "commanding" their appearance on our program. It was a success. Our next production was an Advent service called The Glorious Sounds of The Season (December 2009), based on the text of Psalm 150. Here again we invited choirs, soloists and instrumentalists to represent the sounds, such as the harp, trumpet and strings. We had a real harpist! Our third production was the presentation of Eran McGowan, tenor, in concert (May 2010) with me as his accompanist. Earlier in this chapter I mentioned my presenting two other young talented singers. Eran was no exception. His repertoire also included works of the masters show tunes, secular and spirituals.

"Are we there yet?" you might ask again. "Not quite". I have brought you up to the middle of 2010, but there's one more event I want to tell you about. I want you to come with me to Vacation Bible School (July 2010) while I teach my cadets songs from Galactic Blast, a cosmic adventure focusing on praising our wonderful, incredible, amazing, magnificent, and awesome God. 10, 9, 8, 7, 6, 5, 4, 3, 2, 1 – Here we go. "Blast off!"

When I look back over my life, the song "How I got over" is the soundtrack. You very well might be wondering the same thing – just how did she do all of that? First of all, it was God's grace that brought me through. I firmly believe that he had a game plan for me when I was born. Secondly, I had strong family support. I was the twelfth of thirteen children. It follows that the older siblings helped to care for the younger ones. Some of my older siblings even helped me through college. Thirdly, with help, I was able to pursue a fairly good education. Although I was born in Bessemer, Alabama, I was reared in Gary, Indiana and Detroit, Michigan. I began my music education in the Gary Public School and continued in Detroit where I graduated from Cass Technical High School with a Diploma of Music. I owe a lot to all of my teachers. Later I earned my BA degree from Wiley College in Marshall, Texas (now known as the home of The Great Debaters). After a few years of teaching I spent three summers at The University of Colorado (Boulder) and one summer at The University of Texas (Austin) before deciding to complete requirements for the MS in Education degree from Baylor University (Waco). Finally, I was fortunate to find pleasant places to work. Earlier in this chapter I mentioned the cities where I taught school. The administrative staff and my colleagues in those schools created a pleasant environment in which to work. I enjoyed working with them and I have fond memories of each place.

At this time another question might be running through your mind, "Did any of this gusto for music rub off on your children and other members of your family? As a matter of fact, I like to think it did, because, you see, music is in the family genes. My mother played for her own enjoyment. My oldest sister taught piano and played for churches in Detroit. I had two brothers who played 'by ear'. One on the brothers had a son Leon who sang with The Contours (1960's Motown Records). My son Joseph played trombone in the band during his junior, senior high school and university years. Now he is band director in the Dallas Independent School District. My daughter Angela played flute in the band during her junior and senior high school years. Now she is an administrator in the DeSoto ISD, but she sings with the praise team at her church. Her daughter Ambreal played flute in the DeSoto HS band and marched with them in the Pasadena Rose Bowl Parade New Year's Day 2000. Angela's second daughter Allika played saxophone in the junior high band, but now she plays only for her enjoyment. My niece Marjorie plays classical piano. She was director of the high school a cappella choir before she was promoted to Supervisor of Fine Arts in the Port Arthur, Texas ISD. Her daughter Mollyn who is a lyric soprano, now has the position of choir director left vacant by her mother. Her son Elijah, a tenor, is a singing minister who pastors a Church of Christ congregation is Olney, Maryland. Quite often he precedes his sermons by leading the congregation in singing his favorite hymns. During their high school years in Port Arthur both Mollyn and Elijah won many gold medals in UIL Solo and Ensemble at regional and state competitions. My nephew, Chester, sang for eight years with the Interracial Chorale, a New York City amateur chorus of 150 voices which gave performances at Carnegie Hall, Lincoln Center, and Town Hall. The chorus was also asked twice to sing the Handel "Hallelujah Chorus" for the Easter sunrise service at Radio City Music Hall. The chorus sang with professional orchestras and soloists, including soprano Shirley Verrett, who later became an international opera star. Family members who do not play instrument or sing are patrons of the arts.

When you're young and fresh out of college and you are embarking on your professional career, you don't think about retirement nor do you think about whether or not you will be rewarded 50, 60 years hence. Now that my time has come, there are those persons and organizations who I met along my career journey that thought it would be nice to bestow honors upon me.

The Dallas Metroplex Musicians Association, an affiliate of the National Association of Negro Musicians, Inc. chose me for their 2003 Musician of the Year at their Founders and Scholarship Luncheon. The Dallas Alumnae Chapter of Delta Sigma Theta Sorority, Inc. featured me as pianist for their 2003 Women in the Arts Gala at the Black Academy of Arts and Letters. My daughter Angela was also featured as vocalist. At its concert in June 2004 the South Dallas Concert Choir presented me with a trophy and a certificate of appreciation for 10$^+$ years of participation both as a singer and a pianist. In the field of education the Southeast Dallas Business and Professional Women's Club presented me with the Dreammaker Award for 2004 at their Dreammaker Awards and Scholarship Reception held in December. In February 2006 the Dallas Alumni Chapter of Jarvis Christian College selected me one of the honorees at their Heritage Awards Scholarship Banquet. The United Methodist Women of Community United Methodist Church in Dallas named me Church Woman of the Year 2008.

In closing, I have written all of these pages just to tell you one thing – find out what your passion is and go for it – with gusto!

My Retirement: A Series of Transitions

Marie E. Cowart

For me, retirement didn't happen all at once, but rather it was a series of transitions that all began before I retired- about four years before the official day.

Four Years to Retirement. Sometimes the things you develop can have more than one purpose. As Dean of a large academic college, I knew that I wanted to continue to teach as a way of staying in touch with students and to have a barometer for my College. After an attempt during this year of guiding twelve graduate students through my course in the traditional classroom, I felt a complete failure. Too many people controlled my scheduling calendar. Class meetings were postponed, rescheduled, or substituted by others with access to my calendar. I vowed not to do that again. So I availed myself of the University's distance learning policy. My College offered a degree to students in seventeen community colleges in the state and my course could become a part of that effort. With the guidance of a cheerfully competent instructional designer from the Distance Learning Office and a faithful and knowledgeable graduate student who had taken my course, we spent nine months converting my course: SYP4764 Aging Policies and Services, into a distance learning format. In some of the hardest work I have ever done, that summer I taught the first fifteen students as a pilot, and each following year as Dean I continued to teach sixty students. I thought, I can do this. And I can do this when I retire! My course that was developed to accommodate my role as Dean could also serve in retirement. Little did I know how long I would teach using this new format.

Three Years and Counting. I knew exactly when my retirement day would occur. I had entered the State of Florida D.R.O.P. (Deferred Retirement Option Program) program two years earlier and attended those informative programs for near-retirees offered by the Personnel Office at Florida State University where I worked. I was fully aware that there was limited time- three years- in the formal part of my career prescribed by the D.R.O.P. guidelines. I had the best job in the world – Dean of the outstanding FSU College of Social Sciences – and I wanted to hurry up to accomplish the things I wanted to see happen so the College could continue to grow while maintaining quality into the future. Making the difference in my day job, especially facing a retirement deadline, was a full time endeavor.

While I forged ahead making change - and that we did – I was aware that the all-consuming life as Dean would soon end. As a planner, I needed to be ready for that time as well. I knew I had many hobbies: gardening, cooking, needlework, movies, travel, books, and so on. But I asked myself, was this enough? As a child I had played the violin. During my middle school years I spent some time substituting on the cello and loved that brief experience. So my adventure in preparing for my retirement began. After locating a charming master's student in our School of Music, I spent a year and a half learning the basics, and some of the fun aspects, of cello playing. Music graduates do get fine job offers; too soon my teacher moved away and I was left without the rigor of purposeful daily practice. It took a while, but I learned that the first cello chair of the Tallahassee Symphony lived a few blocks away and not only taught youngsters, but had few adult students as well. This experience was a strong contrast with the first. A well trained cellist teacher quickly immersed me in the classical genre of Suzuki I, II, and III. There were stress-filled recitals and master classes. When I bored of a steady diet of classical, I could fall back on the Appalachian tunes taught to me by my more fun loving FSU alumna teacher. I had developed a love for a personal enrichment hobby to take well into retirement.

Just Two Years Left. I knew that statistically I might live part of my life alone. Women are more likely to outlive men (AOA, 2002). I wanted to address that by extending my already wide social support network in a more formal way. An important part of that consideration was to incorporate fun, service and stronger relationships with women. Joining the General Federation of Woman's Clubs, Woman's Club of Tallahassee was the beginning. This was a natural fit for me as a planner, as the Club owned an historic clubhouse built in 1927 in the historic Los Robles neighborhood of mid-town Tallahassee. The Club was established in 1905, and its historic property harkened to the 1920's Cities Beautiful movement when woman's clubs across the country focused on beautifying their cities through architecturally fine public libraries, parks and other public spaces in order to improve the social fabric of the communities. Participating in the Club was something I could do on weekends and evenings. By focusing on specific projects in the greater Tallahassee community strong bonds were built with other women having similar interests.

Only One Year to D.R.O.P. In building a social network, one thing often leads to another. In building a social network focusing specially on women, other things begin to happen. An FSU colleague who belonged to the Women's Club must have sensed what I was attempting to do, for she took me aside one day and invited me to join her for lunch. Thus my rewarding relationship with the Capital Women's Network began. Although I knew about half of the members, meeting regularly allowed me to meet other women who I am proud to call friends today. Although the Network does not have board meetings or fret about bylaws, it engages in community service by maximizing the members' service interests among each other. Dues are generous enough to allow the group to build an endowed scholarship at the local community college. Thus my goal of expanding my contacts with women was enhanced. At the same time I continued the things I had begun in the three previous years.

D-Day (or R-Day?). I had fulfilled my plan of preparing for retirement. All those required paper work things were completed. To take with me professionally, I had carved out one piece of my career, the distance learning course. I had a new personal enrichment interest, my cello. And I have begun to widen my social support among women. What an accomplishment!

Along with these things, I had booked the long dreamt of three and a half week post-retirement trip for my husband and me. I had prepared two papers to present: one in Tasmania, the other three weeks later in Japan. We had stops in Sydney, Singapore and Hong Kong to fill the time. The trip did what it was intended; I did not think about my (former) work for three and a half weeks. When I returned, my college held a party to mark my retirement. There were faculty, administrators, retirees, and of course, students. It was held in the same building where thirty-five years earlier I had my first FSU Office: Dodd Hall. Surely, I had come full circle. Retirement was going to be a snap. I was ready!

So What Happened? The suitcase was un-packed. The travel clothes laundered and put away. Groceries filled the refrigerator again. It was six-fifteen in the morning. I had overslept. Normally I am up at six sharp. I had things to do. What were they? I knew I had to accomplish some-thing. But I didn't know exactly what it was. I had kept an office at the university; I went in faithfully twice weekly by 8:30 am. That was so I could get parking. I had correspondence to take care of, a manuscript review, and several letters of reference. I wrote a chapter, and did the required library re-search. Yes, I could keep busy. There were faculty meetings; I didn't need to go to those. I wasn't even on the call list. I listened to speaker presen-tations. I could take out time for lunch and still go home early; there were things to do there, too. At night there was a board meeting. Yes, there were things I had to do. I must fit in a time for exercise. And when I took a day off, I felt so guilty. I missed a meeting, my calendar was a mess. I lost my lists. It took too long to run all those errands. I used to do them all on the way home and still prep for dinner on time. I need to get organized again. Aha! There is a meeting in Rio I can go to! Tomorrow I'll prepare the abstract. Then the Power Point presentation needs developing. I'm so busy; I don't have time to accomplish anything. My once well-honed time management was all a kilter. My life is a mess. I was focused on what Atchley describes as the "busy ethic" (Atchley, 2004, 258).

Taking stock was not a one-time thing. I reviewed my activities in retirement almost quarterly in an attempt to get more balance and at the same time achieve a feeling of purpose in life, service to others, and quality in relationships with friends and family. I elevated the community organizations I was involved in and dropped those where I was not making a contribution.

About one year into retirement I held a half-time job with a new employer for six months. This gave structure to my life and helped me to appreciate the time which was mine and that which belonged to my employer, something I had not given much thought to previously when work involved 24/7.

I expanded time for exercise and family. High priority was time with my cello, my family and the two women's groups that I had joined. Everything else had to fit in with the time available. Still, where was the time to read, to garden, and to organize those photos from trips taken each year? Those were the things that I wanted to accomplish in retirement.

I'm not sure when I began to feel less guilty. But slowly it became fun to sleep until seven, instead of getting up at six-fifteen. Adjusting to retirement seemed to come in baby steps.

Three years was a marker for me. I could stay home all day, work in the garden, prepare a nice meal, have a glass of wine, and not feel guilty. I no longer rushed off when stopping to speak to a friend. I even had a second cup of coffee. I serve on boards and committees where my skills are put to use. Because there are fewer outside activities, each gets more of my time and attention. I go out of town twice a month, just to get away. I no longer give papers or worry about going into the office on a regular basis. My calendar has holes in it, for reading, or just taking a nap. My life is full - full of purpose, full of family and friends, full of leisure.

Did all of that pre-retirement planning pay off? It has been seven years since I retired. I am in the tenth year of teaching my distance learning course, this spring one hundred and thirteen students can work whenever they choose throughout a week, and I can respond as my schedule allows. My cello is a constant companion, providing music for personal enjoyment. I continue to work with the Woman's Club, focusing on long term planning, establishing an endowment for the preservation of that historic Tallahassee treasure. Capital Women's Network has evolved into a strong support network, particularly in the past two years when my life partner, Jim, suddenly died. They helped me join a weekly support group, another women's gathering that has given me endless hours of companionship and encouragement. Pre-planning provided things that have stayed with me through the many transitions of this phase of my life, of which retirement is just a part.

I began by saying my retirement was a series of transitions. In pre-retirement I focused on planning rather than separation from my fulfilling work. A trip provided a short honeymoon after which I neither settled into an immediate retirement routine or a period of rest and relaxation during which I did nothing. Neither did I become disenchanted or feel a sense of emptiness. It took me quite a while to begin to reorient and take stock; it was not until the third year that I had settled on a comfortable routine after exploring several avenues of involvement. My routine now is that of a full time retiree with the exception of teaching once a year for four months and serving on several community boards. I am planning to downsize and relocate my home to allow for a simpler life that will allow me time to accomplish my other long term goals; sorting those photos and reading.

Other Thoughts. Another aspect of retiring worth mentioning is that of finances. As a university employee with almost 40 years of tenure in the public system, my retirement income was generous. It consisted of a state pension check, a stipend for supplemental health insurance, and social security. Although my husband and I had ample income, and a nice cushion of savings and investments, there was still a different feeling about money. A finality of resources was felt. No longer would we be saving and stockpiling and amassing wealth without depleting it. Our generous pension income was less than our working income. Maybe we should watch our spending more carefully. We wanted to be sure that our cash flow for monthly routine expenditures did not exceed our retirement income. It took about two years to make this adjustment. When my husband died five years into retirement, I went through another income adjustment, but this time I learned to make the accommodation in much less than two years.

The other aspect of adjustment in retirement that I want to address is caregiving. I had read about people in their seventies caring for relatives in their nineties. Never did I dream that this might happen to Jim and I; much less would it apply just to me. Much earlier we had cared for Jim's grandmother in our home for six years. So the family saw us as caregivers.

When Uncle Tom had a stroke, he and Aunt Helen turned to us since they had no children. We began with transportation and financial management. They lived in an assisted living facility in Miami, 500 miles from Tallahassee where we live. After Aunt Helen died, Uncle Tom, then eighty-six, turned to us just as we retired and had planned a semester of teaching in London. We got the phone call, "Come get me. I need to move to Tallahassee to be near you." Needless to say we cancelled our extended visit to London and drove Uncle Tom to Tallahassee and an assisted living community a few blocks from our home.

As we cared for Uncle Tom for almost five years before his death, Jim's mother in her ninety's was becoming more fragile in Miami where she lived independently without relatives and only a few elderly friends. She had difficulty with decision making, shopping, driving, and travel. There was also her resentment that we had not relocated near her and her brother was getting lots of our attention. With failing vision she knew that she would not be able to pass the vision test for driving, so Jim arranged for weekly transportation to the grocery store and doctor. A neighbor took her to church. Other than those essential trips, she was housebound. She would not use a taxi. Neither would she consider relocating to Tallahassee to be near her brother, her only child – my husband—and her grandson. So Jim began monthly trips to Miami to buy groceries, toiletries and other essentials that she could not manage alone.

When Jim died, I took over those trips, which were pleasant, until one day she fell in a malfunctioning elevator and broke her hip. Still dealing with the grief of my loss, I began 19 months of extended stays and regular travel to Miami. Those trips involved supervising the in-home caretaker, grocery shopping, preparing two weeks of freezer meals, and trips to the doctor, therapy, x-ray and other essentials. Nine months after breaking the first hip, she slid off her bed and broke hip number two. Another surgery resulted in her having a stroke, and later breaking her arm. Needless to say, going home to her condo was out of the question. Now my trips involved visiting and interviewing staff at multiple nursing homes, and settling her into a new routine while avoiding a direct response to "When can I go home?" And so, at age ninety-seven, she became a nursing home resident, and I spent my time in Miami downsizing a condo with forty years of accumulations.

Monthly visits to Miami for a few days were not adequate to supervise my mother-in-law's care in the nursing home. So, I turned my attention to moving her to Tallahassee. I began with a series of interviews of nursing homes and was able to contract with one for a bed within a three to four month window. Once relocated, her visitors consisted of me and her grandson seeing her every day instead of once a month. Some of the nursing staff had been my students. Need I say, her care was exceptional. We had quality time together until her death, unfortunately, too shortly after moving to Tallahassee. Much is written about the burden of caregiving. For me, the burden was lifted. I was in my sixth year of retirement, two years after losing my husband, alone without my partner and facing a new start without the responsibility of caregiving.

This is not the end of the story however. In less than three years, I had experienced three deaths: Uncle Tom, my husband, and my mother-in-law. With death begins the series of trips to the lawyer, court proceedings, resolving property issues, working with beneficiaries, keeping records, cancelling services, and paying bills. None of this happens quickly. Previously I had settled my father's and step-mother's estates. Still, the process of resolving property sales, overseeing funds, and distributing assets takes time and there are unforeseen delays. Estate management has become my part time job.

With everything there are lessons learned however. I am determined not to have my children go through the experiences of caregiving and estate resolution that I have. I have given much thought to planning for my own care and the resolution of my estate. With the expert help of my attorney and accountant, I have consolidated my funds, accounts and insurance. Each year my sons and advisors receive an updated inventory of my assets and belongings and their location along with critical contact information. My pending move to a continuing care retirement community frees me of household responsibilities and my children from having to locate an appropriate facility when I have declining health.

As I look back, pre-retirement involved some proactive steps on my part. In the six years after retirement, I had less control over my actions as other needs arose. Now, once again, I am entering a new proactive phase. The transitions of retirement seem not to end. Perhaps the transitions associated with retiring are just a part of the transitions of life.

References

Administration on Aging (2002) Profile of Older Americans. www.aoa.dhs.gov

Atchley, R.C. & Barusch, A.S. (2004) Social Forces and Aging, 10th Edition. Belmont, CA, Thomson Publishing Company

Achieving Real Gusto through a Career in Entrepreneurial Experiences

Lucy Ho

I am very honored to have been included in this publication, and have requested a friend and colleague, Dee Beggarly, to tell my story. Lucy Ho.

天下為家于挽新知繼流長　海外作客心懷故國思源遠

Hakka Poetry

As a "guest" overseas, my mind is in the motherland and our remote origin,

Making my home globally, I hold hands with new friends to keep our heritage for generations to come.

Siu-Leung Lee

"Hakka Women are characterized by their strong personalities of sharing most heavy labor in the family. They did not bind their feet and fought side by side with men for centuries. (*Asiawind.com*) "

Lucy Ho is a Hakka woman.

The strengths and trademarks of her ancestry have dwelt within Lucy Ho and have been a significant factor in her continuing successes as an entrepreneur within two realms – as a costume designer and restaurateur entrepreneur.

Lucy began her professional life in 1953 in Taipei, Taiwan. Upon completion of her studies in dress making, tailoring, and draperies from Trebien Dressmaking School, she obtained her business license and opened *Lucy's Dressmaker's Shop*—a custom dress design and construction shop whose main clientele were Americans, Europeans and military families stationed in Taiwan. She maintained the shop even after her marriage to John Ho and his departure to the United States to enroll in Indiana University as a Ph.D. candidate in Anthropology.

In 1963 Lucy joined John at Indiana University. Lucy's talents were soon known across campus and she sewed dresses for the wives of the President and deans of Indiana University. With her reputation as an excellent seamstress in place, the School of Music offered her a position in the opera program where she constructed costumes and worked under the direction of established Italian designers. This initial experience in costume construction was the impetus for Lucy to enroll in Indiana University where she studied History of Costume and Costume Design.

In 1965, Gem-Mei Chin Lee, Lucy's mother, arrived on campus at Indiana University from Taiwan with Lucy and John's two children. She had provided the necessary care and support of her grandchildren during these difficult and transitional years. Lucy gives great honor to her mother and readily acknowledges that she could never have been successful in any of her endeavors without the love and support of her mother. From her earliest leadership and encouragement in her young daughter's education, Gem-Mei Chin Lee was a constant source of strength and collaboration. She remained a revered and vital family member until her death.

In 1967 John accepted a faculty position at Florida State University and moved to Tallahassee. During this time, Lucy continued working at Indiana University and raising their two children. It was a year later that the family was reunited in Tallahassee where they have lived since. With Lucy's love of cooking and culinary training, she began cooking demonstrations in her new Tallahassee home. Her students encouraged her to take her talent a step higher. She did. In 1970 Tallahassee's first Chinese/Oriental restaurant, *Lucy Ho's Bamboo Garden* opened. This flagship restaurant has been joined by five other restaurants in the Tallahassee community throughout the last four decades. Her latest is AZU (2009), an upscale Asian cuisine restaurant located on Apalachee Parkway.

In 1969 Lucy's expertise and work ethnic followed her to her new Florida home as the Dean of Indiana's School of Music personally contacted then Dean of FSU's School of Music, Dr. Wiley Housewright. As a means of enhancing FSU's opera program, Dr. Housewright created the position of Costume Designer within the FSU opera program especially for Lucy where she has maintained an unchallenged and esteemed career for over 40 years. Lucy has been recognized for her costume design, construction, and fabric selection. Her costumes, truly works of arts, were placed on exhibit in City Hall in

1995 ("The Dressing Room").

Lucy retired from FSU in 2003, or so the records indicate.

"Retirement" has in no way diminished Lucy's work ethic, energy or abilities. Her work as costume designer and seamstress continue to enhance the nationally ranked opera program at Florida State University. Her costumes have held center stage at *The Florida State Opera* for approaching 100 productions.

Since "retiring," Lucy has been instrumental in opening two of Tallahassee's finest Asian cuisine restaurants, MASA's (2005) and AZU (2009). Not bad work for a retiree!

Lucy's energy and hard work aren't relegated to opera costumes and restaurants. She is surrounded by numerous friends and colleagues not only from Tallahassee, but also from throughout Florida, the nation, and literally, the world. She is a constant when dignitaries, ambassadors, and visitors from Japan, China, and Taiwan visit the Sunshine State. She is well known at the Capitol. Past and present business and philanthropic memberships include:

- **Commissioner, Overseas Chinese Affairs Commission**
- **President and Honorary Chair of North Florida Chinese Association**
- **Board of Directors of Tallahassee Junior Museum**
- **Committee member of Planned Parenthood**
- **Tallahassee Committee member of the Park Service**
- **Member of Florida Economics Club**

- **Member of the Rotary Club of Tallahassee**
- **Member of the Committee of Ninety-Nine of Tallahassee**
- **Board of Directors of Tallahassee Symphony**
- **Board of Directors of Cultural Resources Commission of Tallahassee**
- **International Student Committee at Florida State University**
- **The Opera Guild of Tallahassee**
- **ZONTA (professional woman's club)**

Honors and awards presented to Lucy Ho:
- *2008* **-- Named one of the** *25 Women You Need to Know in Tallahassee,* **recognizing women in business and the broader community who have made an impact on our State and community;**
- *1999* **-- Nominated as "Volunteer of the Year" by North Florida Culture Resources;**
- *1995* **-- Appointed as advisor of the oversea Chinese in Florida by Taiwan Government, Republic of China;**
- *1995* **– Costume as Art Exhibition in City Hall   and Governor's Square Mall, Tallahassee;**
- *1989***—First woman inducted into the Tallahassee Rotary Club.**

One might not be surprised to learn that Lucy admires Julia Child, mid-20th Century TV celebrity chef and author, and has studied her cookbook, *Mastering the Art of French Cooking.* Another Boston celebrity, Joyce Chen, has Lucy's admiration as well. Like Lucy, Joyce Chen was a female Chinese expatriate; opened a restaurant (Joyce Chen Restaurant); and taught Chinese cooking. Chen later published her influential cookbook, *The Joyce Chen Cookbook.* All three of these women share the true entrepreneurial spirit and found success in what they love.

Lucy's yet to be completed dream? Publishing a cookbook, which would offer "secrets of good cooking?" Because as a young woman, Lucy lived in Japanese occupied Taiwan, she has a strong Japanese influence in her recipes and dishes. This also accounts for her fluency in speaking Japanese – a skill she has put to excellent use in her diplomatic and international responsibilities.

If there could be one motto for this Hakka woman it would be: Work hard but always share. Her ancestors originated in the Yellow River area of mainland China thousands of years ago. The Hakka take great pride in their ancestry and from this ethnic group has come influential Chinese as well as *internationally* prominent people – a result of their diaspora. During the last century, descendants of the original Hakka people have migrated to South East Asia, East Africa, Holland, United Kingdom, France, Germany, Brazil, Trinidad, Canada, Australia, Japan, Hong Kong, India, Egypt, and the United States. Hakka people have to fight the forces that attempt to dilute and dismiss their cultural characteristics of language, foods and customs that began about 2200 years ago. The work ethic that is thousands of years old thrives within Lucy Ho. She encourages her children, grandchildren and other relatives to "stay busy – look for new challenges – attempt new endeavors and experiences."

While she enjoys her busy retirement, she still finds the time to share life with her husband, John, her children and grandchildren. Her biggest retirement problem is learning to postpone "YES" to so many requests for help.

Her "hobbies"? Sewing and cooking of course. But also add to that anything that includes "handwork." Lucy recently made over 100 origami boxes for her colleagues at the College of Music. (Origami is the art of creating a symbolic shape by folding paper without cutting or use of glue. It was first developed by the Chinese, but was later adopted by the Japanese.) Her skills have no limitations!

Education has always been an important part of Lucy Ho's life. Her thirst for knowledge has yet to be quenched. She supports education through many avenues – helping local members of the Asian community learn English, funding scholarships for graduate students, and feeding hungry college students on a daily basis. Her goal is to promote Tallahassee as a welcoming and supportive community so that others will want to call it "home." She is a "bridge" for strangers to become friends and residents of Tallahassee. She is persistent in her philanthropy. She teaches and encourages family and friends alike to give of oneself to others. "To share" allows for a greater awareness and discernment of not only oneself and Life, but also allows for personal growth from diverse and humanitarian experiences.

Lucy Ho is the personification of entrepreneurship. To be a successful entrepreneur, one must have passion, a vision and take action. Tenacity and problem solving are daily requirements. An entrepreneur typically takes on what the general population sees as "risky." *Risk* to the entrepreneur is to be calculated and viewed within their self-confidence, abilities, imagination and hard work.

Lucy never allows her hands to be idle – cooking, sewing, origami – something is always happening when Lucy is present. Through her studies and education, her willingness to set aside immediate gratification for long-term satisfaction and success, and her passion for Life, she is a role model like no other. While she does not readily speak of the hardships she has faced on two continents, one only has to imagine the seemingly endless hours of family and professional responsibilities both in her homeland and on "foreign soil." Her smiles, shyness and humility belie the strength, endurance and tenacity that are anchors in her business and professional world. To the frightened student 10,000 miles from home, the colleague who finds a deadline impossible to meet, the neighbor in need, or a struggling business associate, what is seen when Lucy approaches is compassion, heart, and the ability "to get things done." Her generosity and compassion are legendary and leads the way for her vibrant spirit to shine.

As described in the opening Hakka poem, Lucy Ho makes her home far from her motherland, but as she holds the hands of new friends, she keeps her heritage of strength, determination and action alive and well for the future of her adopted and loved home – Tallahassee, Florida.

The Tallahassee community and Sunshine State have benefited greatly from Lucy's motto and advice to her family: "Work hard but always share." Work hard with and for your family. Work hard in educating yourself. Work hard in pursuing your dreams. Work hard at giving back to others.

Lucy Ho is a part of the fabric of Tallahas-see. Tallahassee is stronger and healthier for "holding hands" with a great entrepreneurial woman, Lucy Ho. Fortunately for the community and State, retirement has yet to even slow her down...although she may have to sit still to work on her cookbook.

Traveling through Life with Gusto!

Joel Dawson

GO N 2 GO is on my license plate. If you say it fast, you hear "going to go" which is a good way to describe me at home and when I travel. Once my grandson said, "I didn't know Mo and Pa were going on a trip. " And his Dad replied, "Well, they're in Tallahassee now, so they must be going somewhere."

I have traveled to about 70 countries, many of which were before I retired. My life isn't much different now except I can take more and longer journeys. How did I get the interest in seeing the world? I mainly attribute my wanderlust to my mother. She felt that traveling to all the states was an important part of our education, so every summer we headed out to explore a different part of the United States. We always camped because it was cheaper, and we could be right in the middle of some of the most wonderful parts of our country. Traveling was in my blood. My grandmother took a tour around the world when she was eighty, and my mother and her sister sailed to Europe in their early twenties. I always remembered my mother saying the Amalfi coast was the most beautiful drive she had ever taken. I had the chance to see a large part of Europe when I lived in Munich where my first husband was stationed in the army, but I didn't get to Amalfi until after I retired. It is spectacular!

I guess I have always been a risk taker, always ready for adventures. I grew up in the country outside of Cincinnati where my sisters and I would run barefooted on cinders, climb way up in trees and have mud fights in the pond. Our parents didn't stop us, so we weren't conditioned to be afraid. Also, when we wanted to find something out, our mother would say, "Go ask that person over there." As a result of lots of "asking" practice, I am not hesitant, but eager to interact with people I meet on my travels. Sometimes my interactions might have been a bit stupid. As a young adult I jumped in with a truck driver when hitchhiking in Greece. Another time, I got into a car with four men in the inner city of Denver when I was experiencing the "wilderness" of the city as a member of Outward Bound. I guess I was lucky not to be harmed.

I always participated in sports, staying after school most every day in high school to play field hockey, softball, basketball, and volleyball. I competed in diving and liked to shock people at Y family camp by coming as close as I could to the diving board without hitting it. As an adult, I played tennis, soccer, and then racquetball which I still play every week. I also participate in exercise classes several days a week. These activities help me to stay physically fit which I need to be for the kind of traveling I like to do.

My professional life was always filled with adventure. I had a new job every three to four years.

Why? Sometimes I moved with my husband, other times I was recruited to do another job, or a few times I actually chose to apply for a new job. I was willing to take jobs that I wasn't prepared to do. I never wanted to be a principal, but I did that twice, both times in very difficult situations. I was the first principal of the first local alternative high school, SAIL. We had nothing but a leaky building to start with and had to struggle to get furniture and books, and to keep the school open. In the third year the superintendent even threatened to close the school in three months. I told him my job was to do what is best for the students and mounted a PR campaign to keep the school open. It was successful. Much later in my career I was finally in a job that I was trained to do; I was science coordinator for the district. I was taken out of that job to become the principal of an elementary school where the principal had just been removed. In my career I had fifteen different jobs and I was only prepared for five of them. For all of the rest I was way out of my comfort zone to begin with. By the time I felt comfortable with the job, I was thrust into a new one and a new challenge. I had to work hard to keep up and I think, by nature, I am a workaholic. I always want to do my best. I was cursed and blessed with a strong, adventuresome, and goal-oriented mother, so I always felt compelled to plan and produce.

I didn't know how I would adjust to retirement since I am a workaholic. But I never looked back. I have been very happy in my retirement. I think I just transferred my busyness and planning to a new set of adventures and projects.

I am lucky that my husband, George, shares many of my interests. We both enjoy nature, photography, and traveling to the far corners of the Earth. In retirement we have had more time to pursue these interests. Locally, we like to canoe and photograph the wildlife. We take lots of photos and then spend hours at the computer deleting most of them and enhancing the remaining ones. Each year we choose a few photos to enter into local photography contests. I have been fortunate to have photos selected for the Tallahassee Photofest each year for the last six years, and I have won a couple of prizes. Three years ago I included having our own photo show on my list of things I wanted to accomplish. George and I were selected to have a photo show at City Hall. Last fall we displayed forty of our photos in a show called "Faces Around the World". And now several months later, we attended a nature photography conference in Reno and then skied at Lake Tahoe.

When I am in town, I enjoy entertaining at our home that I designed for that purpose, spending time with family and friends, and working in my garden. I really like reading and then meeting with my book club to share reactions to the book and lifetime experiences related to the book. I am a member of Zonta International, an organization that promotes the improvement of the status of women and girls throughout the world. For years I have done the directory and have headed up several committees. I participate in the beautification committee for our neighborhood and each season I do my part by planting flowers at the street. Having a pleasing and interesting yard is one of the things I like to work toward. And we are lucky to have a pond in our back yard where we can observe the wildlife. Our friends ask and we wonder why we want to leave such a lovely setting so much of the time. It's hard to explain. We always say we are going to stay home more this year, and then exciting adventures present themselves and off we go.

We think about photo ops as we plan a new trip – exotic wildlife and people as well as beautiful scenery. We aren't much into cities. We had a super experience when we went to Arches National Park for a photography workshop. We were up in darkness to get situated for taking pictures of amazing arches as the sun started to highlight the area. We would stay at one spot for a couple of hours and take hundreds of photos as the light made each shot a little better or different. In this workshop we also had the opportunity for our photos to be critiqued by the experts and our team members.

Often we really haven't thought of traveling to a certain place until friends tell us about special experiences they had there or we see something on TV or read about it in *National Geographic*. Our friend, David, showed us photos of a New Guinea Sing Sing where people decorate their bodies as an art form. We just had to go to see the carnival of colors and designs and to experience the music and dancing. New Guinea is probably the most memorable cultural encounter we have had. Just eighty years ago hundreds of thousands of people in the highlands were still living in the Stone Age. They are modernizing quickly, but you can still visit villages in New Guinea along the Sepik River that have no plumbing, no electricity, no stores, no running water, and are a couple of days' paddle to the nearest health clinic. I particularly remember the dishes sitting in a puddle of dirty water waiting to be washed, the scars of induction to manhood decorating a young man who held a falcon as a pet, the chalky clay covered face of a boy who silently watched us as we disembarked our small airplane, the naked little children who served as our volunteer porters, and the brilliant smile of Natalie, a young teenager. One of the things that drives our travels is learning about the extraordinary lifestyle differences around the world and at the same time seeing the universal similarities of music, dancing, love, family, and children playing.

Adventure calls! In Peru I shot a blowgun and stunned the locals when I hit the target. At the primitive lodge in the rainforest it was really black and muggy at night since there was no electricity for lights or air conditioning. We caught Piranha fish for our dinner and were greeted with a large tapir walking through the dining hall. After we visited the awe-inspiring Machu Pichu we headed back to Lima for a final Peruvian adventure - parasailing off the cliffs several hundred feet over the Pacific Ocean. It was rather scary, but exhilarating to run off the cliff and hope to go up rather than crash into the chilling ocean. I did go up and it was exciting to fly over the sea and around the buildings of Lima.

George wanted to go to the Antarctic. It wasn't on my bucket list, but I went along to see what the fascination was. The Antarctic was absolutely fabulous. It was so much fun to walk among thousands of penguins and to hold conversations with them. The Gentoo penguins would come right up to us and squawky talk. I felt as though they were talking right to me. The scenery was spectacular. I particularly remember the day when we were farthest south. It was a brilliant sunny day.

Our Zodiac motored through exquisitely patterned and shaped icebergs, and snow-covered mountains glistened in the background. One of the huge icebergs looked like MacDonald's twin arches. We got out on a tiny bit of land and peered over a wall of snow to see a dozen seals lounging just a few feet away. The whole Antarctic tour was a magical experience. One more trip of a lifetime! When we were on this trip George told several people that we wouldn't be home for a week before I would be planning another trip. At 10:22 AM on the fourth day, I said, "This is probably not a good time to bring this up, but I have been thinking of taking a trip to India." He didn't want to hear about another trip at that moment. I reminded him that you have to plan ahead, or you might not be able to get on the tour when you want. The next spring we went to India!

Have you ever thought what it would be like to have a leech sucking your blood? In northeast India I found out! To find Gibbons we walked through wet leaves that were crawling with leeches. Every few steps we pulled several little leeches off our sneakers. We did get to see and hear the gibbons, but the fee was a leech attached to my foot. I ended up with a bloody sock and foot! In this part of India we also enjoyed visiting our guide's family and seeing how they cleaned the rice they had grown. They were better off than most people because they had a little bit of electricity, enough to power a fan and a few lights, but they didn't have inside plumbing. Their floors and walls were made of cow dung and mud, which made a very hard polished surface. A loom sat on the front porch where the mother wove material for the family's clothing. She gave us beautiful traditional red and white welcome scarves. She learned to weave from the woman next door who was helping women to make some money by weaving and selling cloth.

India was also the location of the most astonishing tiger observation.

We were thrilled to be able to track several tigers during our morning in Rathambhore National Park. A few minutes after we entered the park we came upon a mother tiger and her cubs. The cubs were around two years old. It was time for one of the cubs to go out on her own since she had made a kill by herself. The cub was reluctant to leave, so the mother was chasing it away. They had a horrendous fight in a lake. Water was flying all over the place. They clashed several times before the cub limped off to lick its wounds. I was very lucky to get great shots of this whole series of events. We could have gotten excellent close-up photos in a zoo, but we would have missed learning about and witnessing significant tiger behavior. This encounter was definitely a thrill of a lifetime. Even our guide, a local tiger expert, was concentrating on getting his own best shots.

I push the envelope for thrills. I remember my first ride on the Shooting Star, the biggest roller coaster at Coney Island in Cincinnati when I was around 10 years old. I had my eyes closed as we reached the top of the first big hill. My Dad said, "Open your eyes. Look at the view (of the Ohio River)!" I opened my eyes for a second before we plunged fifty feet straight down. Ever since, I have searched out other coasters to enjoy that exhilaration.

I experienced some special thrills for my 70th birthday. Skydiving was NOT on my bucket list, but

I couldn't pass it up when my husband presented me with the gift certificate. My cute tandem jumper suited me up and gave me instructions. We climbed to 10 thousand feet and prepared to freefall for the first 5000. As I climbed out of the plane, my skin whipped around and I looked like a white-headed smurf with my hair standing straight out. It was quite a rush and then, just as quickly, the parachute opened and I experienced a quiet view of the countryside below. I was met when I landed by cheering family and friends. What fun! Also for my birthday I went go-cart racing – not the kiddie stuff. These carts went at least 50 miles per hour. I drove as fast as I could. I kept my accelerator on the floor except in the turns where I briefly slowed down. I particularly wanted to beat my grandson who is a racecar driver. No such luck. I spun out at a turn. Wait til next time!

Africa brings another kind of thrill. In Kenya an irritated elephant chased us through the brush. When our driver slowed down, we thought the elephant was going to gore our van. Whew, the elephant decided to ease away saving us from disaster. Our hearts finally slowed down to our normal speeds. At the Chobe River in Botswana our driver parked right in the middle of the regular path of the elephants. As a result, I have a super photo of mostly the eye of that elephant. It walked about two feet from me as it skirted our open vehicle. I'm sure the driver was chuckling inside. One afternoon in the Okavango delta in Botswana we did a walking safari. We walked along a path with tall beige grass at the sides. We examined elephant dung and stayed clear of a large bull elephant. I wasn't frightened until the next day when we ventured in an open Land Rover to the same place and drove a little off the road where several lions were lounging. We got right up on them before they were visible. We came so close that we could have bent over the sides of the Land Rover to touch them. Just imagine if they had been hungry the day before. I enjoy these kinds of close calls. They raise my adrenaline and make for a good story.

Another place in the far reaches of the world presented some scary moments. Last summer we flew from Bali to Komodo Island to get up close and personal with Komodo Dragons. Within a few minutes of landing on the island, we ran up on a porch to escape some feisty dragons. At the same time other tourists scurried behind nearby buildings and a ranger climbed a tree to get away from the dragons that were running quite fast in his direction. They are nothing to mess with. Some grow as much as ten feet long and their preferred meals are deer, boar, and buffalo. We humans would make a great snack. Every once in a while someone is attacked by a Komodo dragon.

Recently a dragon grabbed the leg of a ranger while he worked at his desk. Other workers heard him scream and came to his rescue. He didn't die, but was in the hospital being treated for a while. The dragons have large, powerful jaws and their bite is somewhat poisonous and quite septic, so they can be deadly.

The next morning we took a two-hour hike over the island. The only protection we had was a forked stick that the ranger carried. I was toward the back of the line and kept wondering if a dragon was camouflaged in the grass just beyond the trail. We did see around a dozen dragons along the trail and sometimes came quite close to them. We ended our hike by the kitchen where several huge dragons lay in wait. One dragon raced after another that caught a chunk of meat. They might have been running twelve miles per hour, which is much faster than I can run. I photographed one that was moving toward me at a fast rate of speed. Another adrenaline moment!

We like to share our love of seeing the world with our family. We have taken them to the Grand Canyon area and to Yellowstone. When our grandchildren turned fifteen, we took them on their own special trip. We took Troy to Alaska, and Mary Rae to London and Paris because of her interest in fashion. Caleb, who has wanted to be a racecar driver since he was three, didn't want to go on a trip. He just wanted money for a car. Since that was not an option, we took him to a racing school near Chicago. All three of us participated in a one-day racecar driving school. Caleb told us a couple of months ahead of time that he was worried we would race better than he. I proved him right getting the fastest time around the track. However, by the end of the day, he had a better time. He was racing at a track near Lake City before he was old enough to drive on the highway, and now he works for a major NASCAR race team as a mechanic. Maybe the racing school helped to get him started.

We also took the whole family to Kenya since wildlife viewing is our favorite kind of trip. We wanted them to experience seeing some of our favorite animals first hand. Since both George and I started out as biology teachers, we are particularly interested in seeing animals in their natural environment. Animals in zoos are soft and lazy. In the wild they are always on the alert. The zebra, wildebeest, and giraffes take very fast drinks at a water hole before looking up and around for predators. The lions and cheetah, in order to catch their prey, are alert for the young or injured animal. The predators' muscles ripple to give them the strength to attack their prey. And their targets have strong muscles to help them escape the predators.

Of our family, Troy is the one who has become the most interested in traveling. He was disappointed when we didn't ask him to go on our next African safari, and he also wanted to go skiing with us recently. Knowing how much he likes to travel, I am willing him my frequent flyer miles – if there are any left.

Often people ask me, "What are your favorite places in the world?" I can't answer this question without dividing things into several categories. The most fascinating antiquities locations are Greece, Ephesus and Egypt, but I haven't yet been to Petra or Ankor Watt. The best wildlife adventures have been to Costa Rica, Galapagos, Borneo, Komodo Island, Kenya, Botswana, and Kruger Park in South Africa. Later this year I'll be checking out Tanzania. The most outstanding cultural experiences have been New Guinea and India. City highlights are San Francisco, Istanbul, and Rome. The best foreign scenic places are New Zealand, Antarctic, southern Chile, Switzerland, Cinque Terra and Amalfi in Italy, and Iguassu, Niagara, and Victoria Falls. And some of the best places to visit are in our United States: Grand Canyon, Alaska, Yosemite, Bryce Canyon, and Arches, with my favorite natural site in the world being Yellowstone National Park.

Some people would ask why I travel to such "God-forsaken" places. Back to my mother. As a child I wasn't warned against germs, we scraped the ants off to eat the jelly, and I wasn't raised to be squeamish about dirty toilet seats. The adventure is much more important than the cleanliness or comfort of a hotel. I have stayed in some pretty primitive places with an outhouse for a toilet, little or no electricity, no air conditioning and strange food. I have trudged along slippery trails and been caught in violent thunderstorms. But I saw Proboscis monkeys cavorting after the storm in Borneo, watched bread being baked in a clay oven along side the road in India, and got fascinating photos by just getting close and asking people.

So why do I travel so much? I love adventure and variety in life. We rarely return to the same place. There are so many other exciting places, animals, and people to see in the world. I like to learn about different cultures and see the beauty of scenery.

Where to next? Many people our age look forward to returning to France or Italy. We have enjoyed those places, but mostly we don't return anywhere. We will return to Africa to go to some new and some old favorite places. And I'm thinking about Morocco, Madagascar, Thailand, Cambodia, and Kamchatka, Russia where we can be surrounded by bears and volcanoes. And now my sister and I are applying for the TV program, "The Amazing Race". I am counting on being the oldest team ever to be on the Amazing Race.

What will happen when I can no longer travel? I will still explore new ideas and new opportunities near home. Variety and risk-taking bring me that adrenaline rush. I don't get bored, but I think I would if I could no longer enjoy new experiences.

One more thought. You don't have to wait until you retire to travel abroad. Before retiring I had visited close to fifty countries. You just can't stay as long or go as often! I say, "Enjoy life to the fullest no matter how old you are!"

Achieving Real Gusto Through
Managing Existing Financial Resources

Clinita Arnsby Ford

In the words of Jackie Gleason, "How sweet it is". Retirement is so sweet. If only I had known, I would have turned it around; retired first and then worked. The Gusto years are sweet and financial security makes them even sweeter. I found that having financial security could not be the end goal, rather it had to make my money grow and to make it provide the things I wanted. This gives a bit different perspective from when I was working and had to focus on "needs" vs "wants".

If only I would have had the wisdom in my younger years as I now have in gusto. As I look back and think of the College Terrace lots in Tallahassee in the early 50's, selling for $500 each with a $10 down payment and $10/month. The same lots now sell for the upper five-digits. I still have the promotional flyer from the 50's and I get emotional about the golden opportunity that I missed.

One of my first priorities after retirement was to block out the "do-gooders" (those who seek you out to manage your money). I had a financial advisor and portfolio manager who had been with me and served me very well for 20 years prior to retirement. I had no interest in the professional scripts that were presenting so-called lucrative financial opportunities. When it sounds too good to be true it usually is not true. Follow your gut feeling.

When I retired we did not have the D.R.O.P. program that can yield a large lump sum on retirement. We had the "Phase" program that for five years your monthly benefit would be one-half of your regular salary plus your full retirement pay. Together that added to more than my regular salary. That provision was a good financial cushion. I considered it my challenge to make my money work for me and to satisfy my wants. To make the money bring more money I had to make wise investments in a diversified portfolio. Additionally, I had to utilize prudent financial practices that are discussed later in the chapter. Heading the list for me were real estate and an annuity program. Ordinarily real estate appreciates. It's the principle of "supply and demand". Property does not populate. We have all the land we will ever have, thus its value increases. There may be periods of a slump in the economy, but real estate always rebounds. You have to be patient and in position to wait. My second priority was an annuity, that was started several years before retirement. The more you put into it the more you get out of it in benefits. Accordingly, I elected to put in the maximum allowed each month. Yes, it hurts at first, but after a few months of not seeing the money, I did not miss it. Now in the gusto years I am enjoying the benefits.

I considered it important while working to plan for a retirement career. I never planned to retire and sit in a rocker waiting for death. Twenty-one years prior to retirement I became a licensed real estate agent and broker. Later I added to my credentials and became a licensed mortgage broker and a certified housing counselor. Note that all of these are revenue producing and in all instances I am in charge of my schedule and how much I want to work. In my gusto years I do not need someone looking over my shoulder and keeping tabs on when I work. Also, I need the flexibility of travel, which is my passion. I use alternate years for domestic and international travel. With no budget strain I've visited several continents and numerous countries. Further I usually travel alone and make my own travel arrangements. I do not like group travel. To support this habit, every month I have an automatic transfer to a special account which I use only for travel and luxury "wants". This is the fund I use to pamper myself. The gusto years are pampering years.

One of my daily habits is seeking out coupons and retailers' senior citizen discount days or hours. Usually department stores have special senior citizen discount days and eateries have designated hours. This practice is fun and financially rewarding.

I've had past experiences that have been helpful in handling financial resources in my gusto years. When I returned to Florida A & M University after receiving my doctorate I was appointed Dean of the School of Home Economics. That was my first experience with a business budget, financial planning and administration. My second year back I began writing program grants for State funding. Soon I moved into writing federal grants and did this consistently for 25 years. At that point I created an annual national conference focusing on improving the retention/graduation rates of minority students in higher education. This I did for 15 years at which time I retired from the university after 50 years of service there. It was the only job I ever had.

Other experiences include having served a four-year term as National Treasurer of a national community service organization and management of my consulting firm and real estate business. It's simply transfer of learning. You adapt the basic principles of sound financial management and apply as needed.

"Money is the root of all evil, but the source of a lot of good." How often haven't we heard this quote? I am an octogenarian (beyond 80 years young) who can tell you from experience, that the good far exceeds the evil. This chapter will explore the positive phase of how to make money be good to you and reflect on how to avoid financial pit falls.

In your gusto years you want to get the full benefit of the money that you have earned and squirreled away. Moreover we shall look at making money work for you. For many years you worked for money now let's make it work for you. It's important too, to look at "holding on" and not letting money get away from you. You do not want to lose anything. Senior citizens and widows are prime targets of shysters and they are so professional at it. Widows are suspect of having money from insurance and/or the husband left her "fixed". Actually either or both may be true, but you have to keep your guard up at all times. This is the best time to really believe that "if it sounds too good to be true, it's not true". You can save yourself sleepless nights just by being careful and staying alert.

It has been said that women control the wealth of the nation. True or not, what is true is that a number of women who become widows know nothing about their own family finances. They have no knowledge of the family financial accounts, bills, payments or anything. Their comfort is "he always took care of everything and I did not have to worry about anything". If you are in this comfort zone, come out of it ASAP. It is important to your financial health that you know everything and be in position to take over if necessary. It's better to be prepared and not need it than to need it and not be prepared.

Wonder if you have thought about the fact that money has no value? Did that put a spin on you? Sorry, but it's a fact. Value is not in money itself, but is in what money can do or produce. Irrespective of how much or how little you have, money is nothing more than a medium of exchange. The value of money comes when it is used to obtain something.

Money has to be managed. Your spending attitude dictates how you manage money. Prove this by associating each letter in the word "attitude" with its numerical position in the alphabet, get the sum and you'll get 100. Try it starting with a = 1. Management does not mean doing without. In fact it means getting more "bang for the buck". It means that in your gusto years you can enjoy your "wants" in contrast to your working years when you had to focus on "needs". It is in your gusto years that you give events and specify "no gifts" because certainly you have already gotten the things you need. At this point gifts become more things for which you have to find storage space. You just do not need more "things" in your gusto years.

In order to keep on track you need to plan. With no plan you are likely to lose your nest egg or exhaust your savings with little or no value received. Your plan should include both short-range and long-range goals. The short range is to cover those wants that are more or less immediate. The long range is for delayed gratification products/events and for time for your money to work for you. The budget is a plan and very important in the gusto years the same as in your working years. The focus might be a bit different in the gusto years. You are now the central figure as opposed to budgeting a mortgage, household furniture, children's education and retirement. It is now a matter of using what you have and what additional income your money can bring. Don't be stingy about using it for yourself.

It's a matter of personal decision as to what you want to leave behind for your children or other relatives. When I retired I told my children that I planned to spend the rest of my life spending their inheritance. So my philosophy is that I spent unlimited time and money on their education for them to be self-sufficient, I don't need to bother about their welfare when I'm deceased. Believe me I am having the time of my life enjoying their inheritance. Warren Buffet put it another way, he told his children "they were loved but not entitled".

Make your money work for you. You worked for the money so now the money can work for you. You can employ your money by making wise investments. It is suggested that you consult a licensed financial adviser who can give you a personalized roadmap according to your resources, needs and goals. Because there are so many dif-

ferent ways to invest your money it is too danger-
ous to do it alone unless you've had previous experience and up-to-date on provisions and regula-
tions. The one generalization I can share is to be
sure to divest your funds.

Making money work for you can include, but
not limited to, any of the following, singular or in
any combination:

Real Estate Investments: *Top of the list!* Think
of those in real wealth. Two of three did it through
some form of real estate. Do not try this on your
own unless you have experience. It is best to work
with a licensed Realtor. This is no cost to you the
buyer. It is the seller who pays the Realtor. You
may want property for rental or you may want to
invest for resale later. In general real estate appreciates, but there are factors that can exert a
negative effect. That is why you need expert guidance.

Insurance Products: Life policies and annuities
are income products. Your long-term goals will dictate the use of the life insurance policy. At maturity you can continue to pay premiums and let the
policy accumulate in value or you can stop paying
into the policy and allow it to be dormant and accumulate in value or you can cash in the policy. In
case of the latter, the cash in value may be less
than the face value.

Annuities: Wonderful income products especially
if you contributed the maximum while working.
The interest rate on annuities is usually higher than
it is for other products. There are payout options.
Annuities can provide you a (A) one-time lump sum

cash, or a (B) monthly stream of cash for a given number of years, selected by you, or a (C) monthly stream of cash for a lifetime. In option "B" if you outlive the number of years you selected, the payments stop at the time you designated. In option "C" the size of the payments is determined by the number of years you select, the longer the period the less the payments. If you demise prior to using the full amount of the annuity there is no refund. However, if you outlive the number of years you selected, the payments continue for a lifetime.

Stocks and Bonds: Do not try this on your own. By all means use a reputable financial advisor.

Banking Products: This includes such as checking, savings, and certificates of deposit (CD's).

There are several types of *checking accounts*. The banks differ a bit so ask for the folder that explains all of the accounts available at that respective bank. In general as a senior citizen you can enjoy free printed checks, free money orders and cashier checks, free bank box and no checking account fees, to name a few. You also want checking and savings accounts that produce the best interest return. Certificates of Deposit (CD) can be purchased for three months to five years and at specified intervals in between. Do not get the shortest or the longest term. I recommend the six-month CD as an edge against fluctuating rates. Follow your own intuition because when the CD matures and you renew, it renews at the prevailing rate at that time, not the original rate. Thus, follow your hunch.

Once you purchase a CD you are locked into the prevailing rate at that time of purchase until maturity. You pay a significant penalty if you redeem the CD before maturity. You may find at maturity that the rate has gone up or it may have gone down. The CD can roll over, but it does so at the rate prevailing at that time. You have ten days to decide if you want to roll over or redeem. It's all a risk, not of losing the CD, but a risk of what interest rate you can get. That is why I tend to prefer the 6-month plan as it allows you to have more control.

I am sure you already have checking accounts, but as gusto women you are eligible for "free" checking accounts. You can get free checks, too, but these are usually the single checks. I do not recommend those in the gusto years. You need the duplicate checks so you can always have a record of what you have done. You do not need to depend on memory, it's usually faulty. Incidentally, when your checks are printed do not include your driver license number or your social security number. These are portals to theft identity.

In reference to safety and convenience, you definitely should have direct deposit for your retirement and social security checks. Retirement checks that are due on the first of the month are electronically deposited into your account at 12 midnight the day before the 1st. If the 1st falls on a week-end day or a holiday, the deposit is made at 12 midnight of the last week day.

Your bank should provide you with free money orders and cashier checks. If you do not have these perks at your bank, you need to change banks. Some banks give complimentary safe deposit boxes. These are not large boxes. They are rather small. If you need a larger box you can negotiate with the bank to use that small box value as a discount toward the fee for a larger box. Ask for this.

The checkbook should be kept current. Otherwise you may innocently spend what you do not have. This can happen when you rely on the bank balance instead of your reconciled balance. The bank can only account for what has been processed. In reconciliation you must account for all checks written, whether processed or not. When you write a check consider that the money is gone and know that you cannot spend the same dollar twice! Neither should you play the game of writing a check and attempting to time when it will be processed. Electronic processing has cut out that time lapse. In fact in some cases it's instantaneous processing.

Warning, on your bank statement you may see such as; Balance $2500, Available $3000. That extra $500 is not your money in the bank. It is the coverage that the bank gives you for overdrafts. In this case the bank will cover up to $500 in overdrafts, but you still pay the overdraft fees.

Use your checks to help you save. Each time you write a check, round it up in your ledger. I suggest rounding up to the next multiple of five, but you can select any amount as you wish. Example would be a check written for $23.45 in the ledger would be recorded as $25.00. Those extra cents will surprise you as to how quickly they can add up to significant dollars.

How times have changed. Gusto ladies are old enough to remember that in our younger years we were taught to avoid credit. We were told to pay for what you get, do not owe bills, etc. In to-day's world if you do not have credit you are in trouble. Credit is a good item and good to have. You have to manage it and keep it under control. It's the owner who makes credit good or bad. You must handle it with discipline and with a plan. You are to stay in the management position and never let the credit manage you.

Do not fear credit cards, unless you are a loose spender and out of control. Use the credit cards that give you some type reward points. Credit cards are actually good to have. They keep you from carrying around cash and they are more acceptable than checks. More and more retailers are not accepting checks. Gusto ladies do not need to walk around with cash in purses. If the purse is lost or snatched your money is gone. You might get your purse back but not the money. On the other hand, if something happens to your credit cards, just call in the 800 number and the cards are deactivated momentarily. Further if your identity is stolen, usually the credit card company does not charge you. In earlier years you had to pay the first $50.

What kind and how many cards do you need? Be conservative. There are four major cards: Visa, MasterCard, American Express and Discover. The first three have affiliated cards from all kinds of stores, businesses and organizations. Not all retail-ers accept all cards. The commission that the re-tailers pay differs for each card, accordingly the re-tailer decides which card(s) to accept.

Do not charge anything that you cannot pay-out that month. If you cannot afford it, do not get it. Immediate gratification can create an unneces-sary problem. Zero out your credit card balance(s) each month. It's a waste of money to pay interest/finance charges and late fees. Take note of the billing cycle of your cards. You can manage your charges such that they come out on the next billing cycle instead of the current cycle. This extends the time of payment without incurring interest or other finance fees. Sometimes just waiting another 1-2 days to make the charge can give you this advantage of being billed in the next cycle.

Choose your cards carefully. Some have annual fees and the interest rates are not the same. Gusto ladies need cards that are "free" of annual fees and have low interest rates. Beware of the 0% interest cards. Read the fine print as usually that is for a short specified period of time, then the rate sky rockets.

The watchdog of your credit is your credit history kept by three Credit Bureaus; TransUnion, Experian and Equifax. Each is located in a different part of the country and they operate autonomously. You should join a credit monitoring program to keep tabs on your credit history and credit score. The once a year "free credit report" is not adequate. It does not give scores. You need to keep up with your scores as well as your history. Your credit score can be your gate entry or your gate keeper for major business transactions.

The Credit Bureaus do not make judgments as to your credit worthiness. They only compile data submitted to them and produce a score. This is one reason why you do not get the same scores from the bureaus. Another reason is that the bureaus work with what whatever data are submitted to them. All do not have the same data. It depends on what businesses are reporting to the bureau. The three scores are not averaged to produce your score. It is the middle score of the three that becomes your score. A general interpretation of the credit score is as follows:

500's and below = Poor
600's = Fair
700's = Good
800's = Excellent. 850 is the highest possible.

If you see an error in your credit history you can get it corrected by contacting the respective bureau(s):

TransUnion: 800-888-4213 www.transunion.com
Experian: 888-397-3742 www.experian.com
Equifax: 800-685-1111 www.equifax.com

In making a correction you must have tangible documentation to support your claim. If within 10 business days the bureau cannot prove its claim, the correction is made.

You do not need to pay anyone to improve your credit score. You can do it yourself. Protect or improve your score by:

- Paying your bills on time
- Paying the full amount due or more
- Avoiding new charges unless absolutely necessary
- Avoiding the addition of new accounts
- Avoiding the offers of "pre-approved" credit cards
- Avoiding "balance transfer" offers

Each time an inquiry is made into your credit history it has a negative affect on your credit score. Some other factors that have an adverse effect include; excessive debts according to income, maxed out credit cards, late payments, charge offs, bankruptcy and foreclosure.

Did you ever wonder how much damage can be done to a credit score by certain actions? The following is a guide taken off the internet with credits to FICO, the company that created the leading credit score:

ACTION	680 Score	780 Score
Maxed-out Credit Card	-10 to -30	-25 to -45
Late Payment	-60 to -80	-90 to -110
Debt Settlement	-45 to -65	-105 to -125
Foreclosure	-85 to -105	-140 to -160
Bankruptcy	-130 to -150	-220 to -240

What you can note is that the same action takes a different effect according to the credit score. Also, depending on the details of individual credit profiles, the same action can have disparate impacts. Examples of what can cause differences are: number of credit accounts, extent of usage of credit card limits, late payments and other conditions. Thus, two persons with the same credit score can show different effects for the same action. The process is very much individualized.

Gusto Tidbits of Financial Wisdom:

- Put a lot of "you" in your spending plan priorities.

- Your money is not endless. You must have elasticity to stretch your money as far as you can.
- Installment accounts have less impact on your credit score than revolving accounts. The latter is as named, rolls over and over, thus seen as more damaging to debt.
- Outlet stores have cheaper prices than the regular store. Designer stores have outlets. However, you have to know that there is a reason for the cheaper pricing, and it is not to show appreciation to the customer. The products are usually there for one or more of the following reasons: faulty construction, close-out inventory or a poor sales item in the regular store. With very careful inspection, you can find good bargains at the outlet store.
- Do not close your credit card accounts. You can just stop using the card, but do not close the account. The reason is that a major part of the credit score is "credit history". When you close an account you have erased part of your history.
- Pay more than the minimum due on the credit card. If possible pay in full each month and avoid interest charges.
- Avoid using debt consolidation agencies. You pay heavily for this for which you can do yourself. The money paid to the agency is money that should go toward dissolving your debt.
- Do comparative shopping. Do not assume that the larger size is cheaper as this is not

always true. Compare unit pricing to know the better bargain.

- Be careful about product look-a-likes. Some of the larger chain stores have their own brands of products, using similar packaging and colors to look like the standard brands. Know what you are putting in your shopping cart.
- Now that the kids are grown and out of the house, you may want to downsize your housing. This can add to a great savings. There is another advantage if you move into a planned community that provides maintenance and yard services. There could be a reduction in property taxes, house insurance and utilities. If however, sentiment rules to remain at the family home, by all means do so.
- In your gusto years there are many benefits available to you. Take advantage of all of them. Do not be modest about your age.
- You've earned the right to these benefits. Some retailers have special days for senior citizen discounts. Seek and enjoy.

Achieving real gusto through managing existing financial resources can be easy if you are vigilant and remain in control.

Achieving 'Real Gusto' by Earning a PhD after Retirement

Linda M. Fulmore

At the age of 54, I made the decision to accept an early retirement package from my high school district in Phoenix, Arizona. The decision to earn a PhD at this point and time of my life was a personal goal. I just wanted the degree and to study, to write and to learn. The ages of sixty, seventy and beyond were in my future and I wanted to still contribute to society (in yet unknown ways) but have credibility. Embracing the decades to come was my goal and I wanted to be happy about being there with no regrets. I wanted cutting edge knowledge and skills about equity, the learning needs of African American children, and educational leadership.

So, in June of 2000, six days after retiring, I moved into the dormitory at Northern Arizona University. In retrospect, this journey that led to that dorm room began many years ago. The persistence to even begin and endure the doctoral process came from a place I didn't comprehend at the time. The foundation for my life was laid by the example of my parents who worked tirelessly to provide for their family on a farm in Modoc, Indiana.

At a recent conference, I heard motivational speaker, Willie Jolly, for the first time. One of his premises was that success in life begins with a dream. As a child I took long walks in the wooded areas surrounding the farm where I grew up. Those early dreams were for happiness and beautiful places; and later dreams to understand and actualize God's purpose for my life and leave a legacy to the world on some level.

Life on the farm as a child was routine and predictable. There were always chores to do on the farm. My primary summer job was the weekly mowing of the lawn. In addition, I helped my mother in the garden and with the canning and freezing of food for the long winter months. Seeing my parents work so hard and maintain focus had a lasting impact on my life. Though I agree that hard work is good for you, hard work while neglecting one's physical, emotional, and spiritual well-being is not good. I watched my parent's, Frank and Elizabeth, age early and perhaps not experience some things that they wanted out of life. They were proud of their daughters and maybe that was enough. However, I'm sure they had dreams unfulfilled and a few regrets like most people.

School was an outlet; my younger sister and I were regarded as good students. I excelled in mathematics and science. Lowell Barker was my mathematics teacher for three years of high school. He was an outstanding teacher and mentor and encouraged me to major in mathematics at Ball State University and become a teacher. And so I did!

We were and still are a family of mathematicians. Though my parents were not exposed to formal algebra and geometry as it is taught in school, they were exceptional problem solvers. My father had to calculate the amount of fertilizer and grain to purchase for the area of land to be planted. He built fences, sheds, and harvested crops. My mother canned fruits and vegetables, jellies, and homemade mincemeat, upholstered furniture and sewed curtains, potholders, and our dresses and coats, often without a pattern. My parents amazingly hypothesized, drew conclusions, estimated, reasoned, used multiple mathematical representations and established 'axioms for farming' without a high school education, hand-held technology, or excel spreadsheets. They were the mathematicians of their time. That innate ability was passed on to me and as a result I have a degree in mathematics and my son, Eugene, also has a degree in mathematics from Florida A & M University. My grandson, Reliza, loves the science of oceans.

I graduated from high school in 1963 and immediately entered college. The events of the next ten years would be significant. It was a difficult transition from relationships with all white friends who mostly lived on farms to now interacting with other African Americans from larger cities in Indiana. It was hard on many levels to fit in and be accepted. In addition, the mathematics department offered few, if any at all, inclusive experiences for me to get assistance and network with other mathematics majors. As a result, I switched majors to Physical Education and minored in mathematics, a decision that kept me from fulltime employment with the Maricopa Community College District in Phoenix, even though I later took additional mathematics courses to earn a lifetime teaching certificate. However, that was not in God's plan.

In 1969, I married and a beautiful baby boy, Eugene, was born in 1972. That marriage ended in divorce and I made my way to Arizona much to the hurt and confusion of my family. The dreaming continued as I wanted a better life for my son and myself. Immediately, I was employed as a mathematics teacher in the Phoenix Union High School District. Again, God's plan was actualized. I had time off to be with my son; I was building state retirement (Praise God) and I was regarded as a good teacher. The year Eugene was born, I did complete a Masters degree in Education at Indiana University/Purdue in Fort Wayne, Indiana which gave me additional credentials and higher salary my first year in Arizona.

It was not until I left the classroom in 1995 that I even thought of pursuing a degree beyond a Masters. Teaching was my passion and enjoyment came in making a difference in the lives of children. My world changed, however, upon leaving a position as Mathematics Department Chair at Central High School and moving to a teacher-on-assignment position at the District Office. Many experiences and professional opportunities came my way that had a profound impact on my thinking and direction and the formulation of new dreams.

In 1996 the district sent a team of educators to Santa Barbara, California for the Equity in Mathematics Education Leadership Institute (EMELI) under the direction of Dr. Julian Weissglass. It was here, working with a diverse group of educators from all over the United States, that I further understood the effects of racism, classism, gender bias, and excessive testing on student learning. Also during this time, I became more active in three national organizations, The National Council of Teachers of Mathematics, the National Council of Supervisors of Mathematics, and the National Alliance of

Black School Educators. Therefore, it was through these organizations that I met other professional African American men and women, many with doctorates, who became my new mentors.

These varied experiences throughout my life instilled a desire to accept bigger challenges and to want more and to do more. Earning a PHD was a logical next step in the reinvention of myself after retirement. The process was rewarding, but there were challenges along the way. For one, I had not read academic literature to a great extent. Additionally, my writing skills were weak. I earned A's in all coursework which came pretty easy. However, I later understood that many university professors are at times under pressure to inflate grades. In retrospect, I had unrealistic assumptions about my ability to successfully complete the comprehensive exams and written thesis. My comprehensive exams had to be repeated which extended my program by one year. Along the way there were family emergencies, vacations, and part time work as an evening administrator at a charter school. One co-chair encouraged me not to work, but my learning style did not allow for extended periods at the library or computer. I needed the breaks!

Writing for the comprehensive written and oral exams is where the rubber met the road. The process forced me to go deep within myself to a place never gone to before to reach and excel in a place I have never excelled before. It was long, tiring, frustrating with unending periods of writer's block. My experiences were typical of most doctoral students except I was retired and a little older.

I felt frustrated, rejected and defeated in having to redo the written and comprehensive exams; it was devastating and I cried all the way home (about two and one-half hours). However, the committee made the correct decision and after a day of self-pity, reflection and rest, the work began again. My committee co-chairs consisted of the Dean of the College of Education (male) and a female associate professor, I being her first doctoral student. It was not until I elicited the help of a high school Advanced Placement English teacher did my writing improve. I did successfully complete the comprehensive exams in 2003 and later defended my dissertation on April 25, 2005.

The primary research question was what do high school mathematics teachers identify as effective practices for African American students to understand mathematics? My study used both qualitative and quantitative methods of data gathering and analysis. The critical incident technique was used to survey 18 high school mathematics teachers. The results produced 128 positive and negative incidents which were categorized into two major themes: student-teacher relationships and instructional strategies. In summary, African American high school students can achieve in mathematics when the National Council of Teachers of Mathematics Principles and Standards for curriculum, instruction, and assessment are incorporated. Additionally, it is important for teachers to establish positive relationships which incorporate fair treatment, close proximity with personal interactions, acceptance of cultural values and world views, and a personal interest in both within and outside of school activities.

So now years later, was it worth it? Yes! My work in the charter school was in part because the principal knew that I was pursuing a doctorate.

Soon after that a local high school district contract-ed me to work with their mathematics teachers. In 2004, I joined a national consulting team. As a re-sult of those contacts, I was appointed secretary of the National Council of Supervisors of Mathematics in 2007. I also served as 1st and 2nd Vice-President, elected positions. In 2010, I was program chair for the 42nd Annual Meeting in San Diego, CA. Addi-tionally; I chaired the Achievement Gap Task Force of the National Council of Teachers of Mathematics which was the turning point for equity discussions within that organization. The friends and profes-sional contacts I've made have been wonderful. To know and work with like-minded people from all over the United States, Mexico and Canada is a blessing.

At my church, I am chair of the Commission on Christian Education. Though I don't have semi-nary training, I am able to assist teachers with pedagogy, lesson planning, student engagement strategies, cooperative learning activities, Bloom's Taxonomy questions, and curriculum development.

Today I travel on the average of once, some-times twice a month, for work, meetings, confer-ences, and pleasure. In 2002, I joined a travel group of educators and have traveled the world. We have toured Italy, Greece, Croatia, France, Germa-ny, Hungary, England, Scotland, Ireland, and South Africa. Two my favorites were the Baltic Sea cruise from Dover, England to St. Petersburg, Russia and a riverboat cruise from Paris to Normandy. This year we are going to Portugal, Spain, and Morocco. The Great Wall of China and so many other places are on my 'bucket list'.

I truly believe that all this is the plan God has for my life. My goal is for the next decades to be spent mentoring, teaching, being a role model, learning, giving back, and continuing to dream.

In a way, I can now honor my mother and father and aunts (Anna Mae and Mary Ellen), and uncle (Clyde). They did not have the opportunity to finish high school and go to college, but they were resourceful and intelligent. They bought homes and paid for them with no 2nd mortgages, cooked without recipes, sewed and upholstered without patterns, farmed without consultants, and saved money without the stock market or 401K's. They took what they had and accomplished so much. It's my turn to do the same.

Going for the 'real gusto' means doing the things you believe you cannot do. It means creatively thinking out-of-the-box. It means rejecting the status quo of how the world thinks one should be, act, and do in the retirement years. It calls for taking care of our bodies, using good skin care products, eating healthy, enjoying children and grandchildren, loving ourselves and being open to having some else love us. It's never too late!!! Additionally, it means realizing that the future is now and all that we waited for and planned for is to happen now, whatever that might be. So if you desire to pursue educational goals in retirement years, go for it with Real Gusto! And finally, dream, pray and listen to God; He has so much in store for you!

Achieving Gusto Amazingly

Charlotte Edwards Maguire

The truth is that I have never retired as a physician, although my involvement went from fifty years of active practice to that of volunteer. I always wanted to use my knowledge and experience to help others. My father, who was a great influence in my life, was a well-educated man with a masters in engineering. He encouraged me to think and analyze and move forward with common sense. He always said: "A smile will make your worst enemy a friend." Growing up loving people shaped my choice of vocation and continues to this day.

Childhood

I was born in Richmond, Indiana September 1, 1918 where my parents, then living in Florida, had gone to attend the funeral of my grandfather. My parents had moved to Orlando from Ohio in hopes my mother, who suffered with diabetes, would achieve better health. Alas it was not to be so. I was seven years old when she died. My paternal grandmother came to live with my father and me. She was a strict Quaker ever attentive to my proper deportment as I grew up. She always lovingly encouraged me and took pride in my accomplishments, especially when I entered medical school. My father, who did not remarry until he was 72 died at the age of 95.

College and Medical School

Upon graduating Orlando Senior High School in 1935, I attended Stetson University, the University of Wichita and received a BS at the Teachers College in Memphis.

The story of how I got into medical school is worth telling. Some of the fellows I was in school with were going to medical school in Tennessee. As more or less a joke, I also filled out the form. Imagine my surprise three months later when, not realizing they sent it in, I received a letter saying I had been admitted. I could not go to the Dean and admit I had done it for kicks so I packed my bags and headed to the University of Tennessee.

After three days at the University, however, I was called into the Dean's office and told that they needed my place for a man and I was permanently dismissed. My grandfather, who was with Northwestern University, was outraged when he learned of my dismissal. He learned that his friend, Dr. A. J. Carlson, who wrote THE book on physiology, was coming to Memphis and arranged for him to meet me. We had a nice conversation but there was no mention of medical school. Dr. Carlson then asked me if I would drive him to Little Rock, Arkansas and back. As I did not have a car he arranged for one and we made the trip. What I did not know was that we were going to visit Dean Cromar, the head of the University of Arkansas Medical School, for whom Dr. Carlson was a mentor. They talked for some time and went out to lunch together. During this time I waited in the room with the Dean's secretary. In the middle of the afternoon, the Dean came out of his office and said: "Miss Edwards, I would like for you to go back to Memphis, pack your bags and be here by Monday morning."

The truth is that I had been somewhat relieved when I got turned out of the medical school at Tennessee. I was delighted to go back to my studies in physics. But I was not going to disappoint my father, grandfather and Dr. Carlson and found myself a medical student at the University of Arkansas.

This was 1940, at the beginning of World War II. As the only woman in the medical school, they did not quite know what to do with me. They assigned me to duties in another building since the professors were more comfortable lecturing to the men. Fortunately, my classmates took notes for me and were very supportive of my being one of them.

What I ultimately discovered was the professors did not feel comfortable lecturing to a woman about men's anatomy, diseases or attitudes. Moreover, they were limited as to women's feelings and responses to diseases or how we reacted in general to illnesses.

I did my share with whatever work there was and helped my classmates understand some of the things I knew. I had been trained in nutrition, chemistry and physics. Slowly my presence began to make a difference. Before I graduated, the professor in obstetrics asked me to help him edit a book. He said he had learned from my comments that he did not know how women felt!

Starting Practice

Following my graduation from medical school, I went back to Orlando where I did my internship and residency at Orange Memorial Hospital (now

Orange Regional Hospital). Once again I was the only woman physician on staff. The Orlando Sentinel newspaper greeted me with the headline: "Orlando's First Girl Doctor Returns."   Even in this environment, I was able to bring new thinking to the practice of medicine. The pediatrician, Dr. Sinclair, who had treated me as I was growing up, saw me one day in the pediatric ward leaning over a baby and whispering. He asked me what I was doing. I explained to him that *in utero* these little fellows hear nothing but a mumble or whisper. If you whisper to them they quit crying. He tried it and it worked and from then on he too was hooked!

Following my residency in 1945, Dr. Sinclair asked me to take over his practice saying he would stay with me as long as he could. The second year of our partnership, Dr. Sinclair died on a boat trip on Lake Apopka and I was on my own. It was early in my practice (1947-1948) that I received a call from Dr. John Tigert, President of the University of Florida, asking me to serve on a committee to establish a medical school at the university. I argued that I was just out a school and perhaps he needed someone with more experience. He said: "Let me tell you why I especially want you: 1) You are a woman and you have been through the mill and will hold your own with the men on the committee 2) There are twenty on the committee, all except you have been out of school for 10 to 20 years. They know little of what is going on in medical education today. I need someone who understands the present curriculum and the attitude of present physicians. I accepted.

In 1948 I married my beloved husband Raymer Maguire. He was a highly regarded attorney and community leader in Orlando, a member of the Maguire, Vorhees and Wells Law Firm that later represented Walt Disney in the development of Disney World. During his distinguished career, Raymer served on the State University Board of Control, the Alfred I. Dupont Institute Board and on the Constitutional Revision Board among others.

Many opportunities to contribute in my field came my way during my years in practice in Orlando. I served on the medical staff of Orange Regional Hospital, directed the Orlando Child Health Clinic, was President of the Central Florida Society for Easter Seals, and on the board of the Central Florida Mental Hygiene Society.

In the late 40s, I had the opportunity to do a residency at Bellevue Hospital and Medical Center in New York City. When I first started my practice, I knew I needed to know more about physical disabilities and mental disabilities. I went to New York for the specific purpose of training under Dr. Howard Rusk, the physical therapy pioneer, at the Institute for Physical Medicine and Rehabilitation on east 34th street, so that I could recognize disabilities and know how to treat them. One of the purposes of the residency was to find all the people in Bellevue (almost 3000 patients) that could benefit from rehabilitation, and because there was no place for a woman to stay at the Institute, I ended up in a room at Belleview.

One of my most memorable recognitions came in 1957, when as Vice President of the Florida Society of Crippled Children, I represented the United States at the Seventh World Congress of the International Society for the Welfare of Cripples in London. I had the rare opportunity to spend a week with Prince Philip who served as the honorary chairman. Meeting others in my profession from 91 other countries was a once in a lifetime experience. My husband, Raymer, accompanied me on this trip. While I was occupied, he attended the American Bar Association meeting in London.

In 1968 Governor Claude Kirk came to my office in Orlando and asked me to come to Tallahassee as an Assistant Secretary and Director of the Crippled Children's Commission of the newly created Department of Health and Rehabilitative Services (HRS). Leaving private practice and Orlando was a difficult decision, and frankly if I hadn't thought this was the greatest challenge of my life, I would not have gone to Tallahassee.

After several months I went to HEW in Atlanta as the Assistant Regional Director of Health and Scientific Affairs at the request of the Director Cary Hall, whose brother was a Florida pediatrician whom I had known. From Atlanta I moved to the Federal Executive Institute in Charlottesville, Virginia for training to prepare me for a high level position in the Department of Health Education and Welfare (HEW) in Washington.

In 1975, I called the Secretary of HRS, Emmett Roberts to ask if he had any place for me in Florida. A few days later my phone was ringing when I walked in the house after work. It was Emmet saying: "Get down here by 8 o'clock in the morning. We need you back here as senior physician for the Department."

Under my purview was a review of all state institutions – mental health, corrections, nursing homes and Sunlands (retardation). I put together a committee made up of another physician, two pharmacists, two environmentalists, two nurses, and two from laboratories. We visited each institution, reviewing medical records, evaluating patient care and the duties of staff. This was a very rewarding position and held my attention until my retirement in 1994.

My retirement did not last long. Quietly resting at my place in the mountains and finding great enjoyment in relaxation, I received a call from the State Treasurer's office asking me to return to Tallahassee and set up a medical office for workman's compensation. He said he needed someone who understood politics as well as medicine.

Those were interesting times. Working directly under the Secretary of Labor, Mr. Wally Orr, I soon discovered that no one could get positive answers as to who approved medical care for workers. I quickly learned that it was other people not physicians who made these decisions. I asked for a computer run of workmen's comp injuries and got a list that took two weeks to go through and evaluate. The person responsible for okaying the payments had no idea what was required to treat diseases and injuries. My report woke people up and the Department got down to brass tacks.

After almost four years, retirement called to me again. I moved to Westminster Oaks, a full service retirement community in Tallahassee. I had no reservations in moving to Westminster Oaks because the committee I chaired as Senior Physician of the Department of HRS years before had reviewed it carefully.

Westminster Oaks has become my extended family for the past 18 years. My immediate family is gone. My husband, Raymer, had died years before in 1960. Our son, Tom, a professor of nuclear physics at Harvard, had also passed away. My great grandchildren are close to me and are a source of comfort to me.

Life since retirement has been full. I am busy from morning to night. It is impossible to do everything that I would like to do. In the 1980's I studied courses in genealogy and became a member of the National Genealogical Society. I used this knowledge to teach courses in genealogy at the Academy at FSU.

As a trustee for the Maguire estate, I felt I should understand more about real estate and so obtained a real estate license. As a result, I am the proud holder of a certificate from the Graduate Realtors Institute.

I serve on the Board of Tallahassee Memorial Hospital Foundation and the Board of the Florida State University Medical School. In fact I was the first benefactor of the FSU College of Medicine, creating an endowment from a savings account I had started as a child. On Valentine's Day in 2002, FSU awarded me an honorary degree – Doctor of Human Letters. President Sandy D'Alemberte, in making the award, stated it was the first time in his career he had given a doctor's degree to a doctor making me Dr. Dr. Maguire.

The students in the medical school have given me many hours of pleasure as I have encouraged young women to enter the profession and played the role of a befuddled older patient upon whom they could use their bedside manner.

Keeping physically fit was always important to me. After moving to Westminster Oaks, I began to observe that the Tallahassee Democrat carrier often threw the papers in the ditch or at the end of the driveway making it difficult for some residents to claim their paper. I decided to become the extra paper "boy" at Westminster Oaks as I took my early morning walk. I would pick up each paper and put it at the door. Just like the postman, nothing deterred me on my rounds, often going out in the cold and the rain, accompanied by my dog, Windy.

Windy came to me quite by accident. She had been abused and at the time I found her was covered with marks of having been beaten. At first she was suspicious of my gentle handling, but over the years she became my faithful companion and now rarely leaves my side.

Painting also occupies my interest and time. Without any formal instruction in painting, I courageously took brush in hand. The walls in my home serve as a gallery for my paintings. Most recently I have painted birds and mammals brought from around the world by a friend, Dr. Dave Redfield. I have been told by more than one discerning eye that I am quite good!

My most recent endeavor is the Maguire Center for Learning at Westminster Oaks. I was fortunate to have the resources to make a gift to the residents which will give them a place for life long learning. My father always taught me that you must give your gifts before you die. It was fine to have a will, but better to share while still alive. The recent dedication was attended by not just the Westminster Oaks community but the broader Tallahassee Community as well.

Everything I have learned throughout my life has bolstered my joy in retirement. It has allowed me to give back to others in ways I could never have imagined when I filled out -- as a lark -- that first application to medical school.

Achieving Real Gusto through Positive Attitude and Behavior

Freddie Groomes-McLendon

Having been born some "X" number of years ago to Negro parents living in a colored community and growing up to be a proud African American woman, "life for me ain't been no crystal stairs."

My life has been a series of special challenges and significant opportunities that I consider an advantaged life. It has been my mode of operation to focus on the positives that convert as many negatives as possible into opportunities of advancement. That has proven to be a lot more productive and often a lot of fun.

Retirement for me has been a new and positive chapter in my life and especially since my goal is to serve, be positive, healthy, satisfied and experience "Real Gusto".

I will illustrate in this chapter some of my life experiences that can easily be defined as challenges and others as opportunities that ultimately worked to my advantage and yielded a modicum of success even when they may have started out as difficult challenges.

I will begin with the fact that I was born the first child to the union of Fred and Lenton Lang. As the first born my father decided to name me after him, Freddie a feminized version of Fred. Not only did I inherit his name but also his malady, asthma. This illness prevented me from vigorous play and involvement that my sister and brother enjoyed. Instead I lived a somewhat sheltered life usually remaining indoors with my mother who did not work outside of the home. Exhaustion and heat caused the onset of an asthma attack. My mother and I usually read, worked puzzles and cooked. From this I developed discipline and good study habits and became a very good student. Was this a malady or a converted advantage? Well life goes on.

I married right out of high school. I became a mother early in life. In fact I became pregnant on my honeymoon. This did not deter me from seeking my higher education degree. My husband had indicated to my parents if they allowed us to marry he promised he would see to it that I finished college. College life was a bit of a struggle but we did it. Eventually with two kids to parent and a husband who was now a commissioned army officer and stationed overseas, I managed to graduate with honors from FAMU successfully, pledge a sorority, earn a scholarship and publish a regular article in my hometown newspaper, Florida Times Union, entitled "News For and About Colored People" (early 50's) in the process.

My first professional job was teaching Home Economics at Havana High School. I was a young teacher and many of the students related to me and would seek me out for counsel before, after school and during my break in the teacher's lounge.

This challenge motivated me to return to the University and pursue a Master's degree in Counseling and eventually a Ph.D. in Counseling Psychology. I felt a need for more than a positive relationship with students, I needed more training. Later I felt a need to become an administrator and a person who developed policies. I noticed that was what was needed to help advance the "disadvantaged students" with whom I worked. They required a new and different approach to teaching and learning that would necessitate policy changes.

Later, I spent some nine years working in Project Upward Bound as a Counselor and eventually assistant Director. This was a federal grant position and did not afford me the job security of a regular state line position. It did, however, afford me some advantages, among which was the option to take courses at the University at no cost. It was this opportunity that allowed me to earn most of the credits for my terminal degree and ultimately I took a one year leave of absence to complete the writing of my dissertation. Another challenging process or an advantage?

After earning my Ph.D., I was made an offer by the then President of the Florida State University Dr. J. Stanly Marshall. He offered me a position that provided the security of a regular state line position that I had wanted. And most importantly he offered me a great opportunity to make a difference in the lives of many. I was appointed the first African American and Woman to serve as a member of the University Council (the governing body of the university). In this role I was to assist the university in responding to the needs of Minorities, women and the physical disabled. This was a very special challenge and I wondered if I or the university was up to what would be required. In conjunction with many responsible faculty and administrators I developed the first formal Affirmative Action Plan for the University. This plan was ultimately designated one of the first Affirmative Action Plans approved by the U. S. Office if Civil rights along with Harvard and MIT.

The implementation of the program required the aggressive leadership of the president and key hiring officials. This proved to be somewhat of a daunting task, but in time I was able to covert many of the apprehensive and often conservative educators at the university that Affirmative Action was truly in the best interest of all. Eventually the University became noted for successes as one of the leading universities in the country in the recruitment of African American students and the leading university in the Country in the area of Affirmative Action implementation as evidenced by a national review and the awarding of a citation by the U.S. Department of Labor.

These observations are revealed here to provide a backdrop for the new and exciting phase of life that I am now enjoying. Yes I am a "Gusto Woman" in retirement and I'm proud to share why this is so.

I officially retired in 2003 from the Florida State University where I had been employed for 32 years and served five different presidents as Executive Assistant to the President. I am told that I am a survivor. I think that's right. I learned to survive many years ago as a child by focusing on accentuating the positive. Retirement can be the best phase of your life if you plan ahead for it. I set short and long term goals for my retirement just as I had attempted to do for my career.

I made adequate preparation financially through personal investments and contributing to a state retirement fund. I did this early in my career even though I was married and my husband had a retirement plan that I could have shared, I felt that I needed to prepare with my own. That proved to be a good decision. After 49 years of marriage my then husband and I divorced. This divorce occurred at the eve of my retirement. What a bomber.

Well, at first I was uncertain as to what to do. Here I was in my late sixties, I had never really courted beyond my husband. I had never lived alone. Wow! What does a grandmother do with this new status and all this new freedom? My response was" perk up," remind yourself just how special you are, reunite with old friends and family, exercise, eat well, travel, spend wisely and render service to others. Service to others is very inspiring and ful-filling for me in retirement.

When you do unselfish deeds for others it is most gratifying and it will take your mind off of what you don't have as you help those who are less fortunate. You become a great contributor and I be-lieve that you are blessed for it. My faith in God has played a key role in all that I have done in life. I consider myself a favorite among God's children and he always protects me and keeps me from ul-timate hurt harm and danger. This does not mean that I never have difficult challenges because I do. But many of them end up as rewards. Retirement requires that you put your challenges in perspective and adjust to a new or different lifestyle.

My divorce after 49 years of marriage is an example. I prayed for years that God would bless my marriage and keep my husband and I together. Well, God had other plans. I was blessed for many wonderful years with a wonderful marriage until things changed. I now think I should have been praying for peace and happiness. I thank God for the good years and I especially thank God for the two wonderful children that came from our union, Linda and Derek. And my late son Derek blessed me with two wonderful grandchildren Derek II and Deriah.

This divorce could have been a crushing experience but let me get on to indicate how this was not all bad. I learned to adjust and move on. Among the things I did early on after the divorce was to return to my hometown Jacksonville for my 50th High School Reunion.

I arrived early to check in at the hotel. It was too early for the reunion registration so I decided to have lunch. As I walked to the hotel's restaurant, I noticed a tall male silhouette coming down the hall in front of me. As the silhouette got closer, I recognized an old friend. In fact it was the young man who had escorted me to my senior high school prom some 50 years ago, my old friend Dennis. We greeted each other with a kind embrace and decided to have lunch together.

Our lunch developed into three hours of conversation and catching up on life. Believe it or not during lunch we both confessed that we both had decided that we would never marry again and would enjoy our lives as singles. To make a long story short we decided to change our minds and were united in holy matrimony one year later. My husband Dennis is the reason for much of my current gusto. He is a very loving, encouraging and supportive partner. My retirement life is full of gusto and the fortune of a great partner.

I have also had to cope with recent losses, the passing of my mother and the death of my only son Derek who was truly the sunshine of my life. The death of these persons in my life recently has motivated me to live life more fully. Tomorrow is not promised, so we must live each day as if it were the last. Leave only those things undone that are not important or that are just not possible to accomplish today. Employ others to help you achieve your goals where possible.

Someone once said, "What you do together no one can do alone". I am involved in many collective efforts. I also think that everyone should find their "own thing" that affords a real aha in your life. It's there, you need to find it. For me service is one of the things that provides the "aha" and gusto in life. I hope to live a long and fruitful life. For me this requires good health, good relationships and good service.

In order to be successful I require several things, I must work to stay healthy. I see my doctors regularly. Yes doctors, all of them, don't laugh. At this stage of life you'd better check with all of them. I see my general practitioner, my gynecologist, my ophthalmologist, my dentist and my physical therapist and others as needed. I exercise five days a week. I walk two to three miles Monday Wednesday and Friday followed by 45 minutes in a senior citizens exercise class. On Tuesday and Thursday, my husband and I ride our bikes for three to five miles. And I routinely get 7 to 8 hours of sleep daily.

I eat healthy meals with reduced fat and salt and eat lots of fresh fruits and vegetables. I choose green tea as my beverage of choice as opposed to coffee and sodas. Oh yes, I enjoy a glass of wine at meals or with friends. I realize all of this is essential for a long and fruitful life. Old age is mandatory if you live long but a good productive, healthy and fruitful life is optional. The option is up to you. It is critical and I think you must also remain positive and believe that the best is in store for you but you must work at it.

In order to remain positive it sometimes requires that you remove negative people and experiences from your life and these negatives are everywhere, so beware. When they're removable remove them or move on. If you cannot, use this antidote of "positive showering them with goodness and good messages." Refrain from entertaining their negativity and for sure don't react to it or entertain the process. Maybe the negative forces will move on. Try it, it's worth the effort.

Good relationships can be a challenge. They take time to develop. It takes time to maintain them. And it also requires good listening skills to encourage them. The easiest way to a good relationship, I think, is to always remember to make the person feel that they are important. Demonstrate respect for their being. This is true of everyone, spouses, girlfriends, boy friends, family members, colleagues, neighbors and even enemies that you may want to rehabilitate. Everyone wants to feel valued and important. So positively work to realize or nurture good relationships. You need good relationships in your retirement years.

And the thing that really consumes most of my non sleeping time in retirement following my

wifely and family commitments is my service involvement. Occasionally, I think it consumes too
much of my time and I am working on how to say
no gracefully and stick to it for some of the request
that are not all that fulfilling. You see, I truly believe that service should be fulfilling. For me that's
the payoff, fulfillment. Currently I am quite involved
in uncompensated duties and responsibilities but
they are most fulfilling. Money truly is not everything in my life today. I don't mean to try and fool
you, money is still a valuable necessity, just not the
all in all that many believe it to be including me at
one point in my young life may have thought.

The truth is that many of my service activities
support my hobbies and areas of interest. I love to
travel and I love people. My service as a member of
the Directorate (governing board) of Alpha Kappa
Alpha Sorority, Incorporated (service organization)
has provided me with extensive travel experiences
in America and abroad. I share in the responsibility
of visiting ten regions throughout the United States
and abroad. I have attended Directorate meetings
that are held here in the states and exotic places in
the states like Alaska and neighboring country
Canada and sometimes even abroad. We recently
had a Directorate meeting aboard a cruise ship to
Key West and Cozumel Mexico. These trips cost me
nothing except time and service in behalf of the
membership. It's a great opportunity for service.

When I served on the Kellogg Foundation
Leadership Board I traveled to many states and
many foreign counties that included Spain, Europe,
Russia, Japan and the Continent of Africa. All it cost
me was my time and service as I tried to make a
difference in the lives of others. I could perhaps

never have afforded some of these experiences and extensive travel, but service does pay. Service may not always pay in travel and living expenses at luxury hotels but it pays in the richness of fulfillment and satisfaction of serving others and making a difference in the world. Someone once told me that service is your payment for living on earth. So why not serve. It really feels good and it gives you something special to get up for in the morning -- other than breakfast. For me it's true gusto.

Some of my service means that I make personal and financial sacrifices. My service as a member of the Board of Trustees at Edward Waters College requires that I am responsible for my travel and related expenses and financial contributions to the College. It is my pleasure to do. I feel blessed to be able to contribute. I serve as a Steward at my Church Bethel AME. I tithe and again I consider it a blessing that I am able to give of my service and resources.

Well I have really shared my life story to a degree but from "whence I come" has determined the beauty of my retirement. And I do consider my retirement a beautiful chapter of my life. I feel I am achieving my goal of a long and productive life with good health, good relationships and good service to all mankind. This is truly my version of Gusto Comes Later. Prepare well for retirement if you're not there yet and Join me in retirement by living with gusto if you are. Retirement can be a wonderful and happy period or chapter of life. Believe me, it can be FULL OF GUSTO IF YOU REMAIN POSITIVE IN YOUR ATTITUDE AND BEHAVIOR. I say, Go forth and live with gusto in your retirement! You earned it, enjoy it.

Recognition of Unfinished Business Injects the Gust into GUSTO

Barbara K. Barnes

At every stage of a woman's professional life there are constraints of time, place, and circumstances that prevent one from pursuing a number of personal goals, interests, and aspirations that may or may not be related to her job at that stage of her career. Have you not thought to yourself at some point in your career that "If I just had the time, I would help this family member, help that colleague, help these students, support this community project, or attend that meeting, conference or event?" I believe that when one looks back over one's career at the point of retirement, one will discover much unfinished business. This unfinished business includes friends and relatives she wanted to spend more time with, "**causes**" she wanted to support, places she wanted to go, projects she wanted to complete, special skills she wanted to acquire, problems she wanted to solve, and issues she wanted to address. This is certainly true in my case.

Let me tell you what happened to me when during the fifteen or so months following my retirement from Florida A&M University as professor in the College of Education. When I reflected in ret-

rospect on my thirty-eight year career as a professional educator, I saw my career as having three
plateaus. The first plateau was the teacher plateau,
the second was the junior administrator plateau,
and the last was the senior administrator plateau.
At each of these plateaus, I led a very active, full,
and rich life as a wife, mother, homemaker, and
full-time professional. This meant that like everyone else I only had twenty-four hours a day to fulfill
my personal and my professional obligations and
have discretionary time for other **"important"**
things, like rest and recreation.

My teacher plateau covers the years when I
taught high school English and Language Arts at
Rickards High School, FAMU Developmental Research School, and Belle Vue Middle School, taught
Freshman Composition and Education Methods
courses at Florida A&M University, gave birth to two
sons, Martin and Marcus, earned my Education
Specialist degree in Reading and Language Arts and
the Doctor of Philosophy degree in Educational
Leadership and Administration from Florida State
University all the while being a homemaker and a
wife for my husband, Malcolm. On this plateau, I
left much unfinished business. There were many
high school and college students that I wanted to
tutor. There were new teacher colleagues that I
wanted to mentor, there were causes I wanted to
support, research I wanted to do, home improvement projects I wanted to complete, educational
enrichment I wanted to provide for my sons, college friends I wanted to visit, extended family I
wanted to get to know, and exotic places I wanted
to visit with my husband.

When I moved from the teacher plateau to
the junior administrator plateau in 1991 upon be-

coming Founding Director of the Teacher Preparation and Career Development Center in the FAMU College of Education, I left behind much unfinished business. While on this plateau my administrative experiences expanded and I became the Director of the FAMU Evening and Weekend College, maintaining my schedule of activities as a mother and homemaker, and broadening my professional exposure and contacts. As our sons were growing up and expanding their activities outside the home and my husband was progressing in his career, there was little time for me to address even my highest priority altruistic aspirations. After busy and intense work days, I eagerly looked forward to weekends, which I could find rare hours of rest and recuperation.

I reached the third career plateau upon my appointment by Dr. Frederick Humphries, President of Florida A&M University, as Dean of the FAMU School of General Studies. By this time I had earned the Ph.D. degree in Educational Leadership and Administration, my career was blossoming, my sons were finishing college and high school, and my social engagements had greatly expanded through active memberships in numerous professional and social organizations, which included the American Association of University Professors, the Association of Supervision and Curriculum Development, the National Council of Teachers of English, the Florida Association of School Administrators, the International Reading Association, the Drifters, Incorporated, Zeta Phi Beta Sorority, Inc., and the Red Hat Society. Before my retirement in 2008, I had experienced three years as the chairperson of the Department of Secondary Education, a combined tenure of twelve years as a Director of two different academic programs, five and one half years as Dean of the School of General Studies, twenty- two years of teaching and research as professor in the FAMU College of Education, had served on the Presidential Transition Team of FAMU President, Dr. James Ammons, and served as his Interim Provost and Vice President for Academic Affairs for seven tumultuous months before my retirement from the University in May of 2008. Suffice it to say that the vantage points of these two senior administrative assignments allowed me to see many administrative problems that needed solving, many more professional development needs of faculty and administrators, and many societal needs, few of which I had the complete authority, the time, nor the resources to address. These limitations were particularly bothersome for me especially when I had firm ideas about how to solve or alleviate the perceived problems. So then on the third plateau of my career, as on the other two plateaus, I left major unfinished business in areas which are of high personal interest and genuine concern to me even to this very day.

When in the hours and days of retrospective reflection on my career that have transpired since my retirement twenty-one months ago, my recollections of many challenges, issues, and people that I had encountered and engaged on each of the three plateaus of my career began to excite my curiosity and interests. I began to recall how I had envisioned addressing those challenges and issue, and how I would interact in altruistic ways with various students, colleagues, friends, and family. I somehow concluded that many of the solutions to problem and challenges that I have conceived still could work and even more than that, I still have the interests and desires to address some of this unfinished business. Above all, I realized that I now have more time and additional knowledge that I can invest in addressing some of my unfinished business. I also realize now that I know many former colleagues, friends, associates, and family whom I may be able to engage in helping me take care of some of my unfinished business. Why would I think that any of these people would be interested in helping me take care of my unfinished business?

Well, there are two reasons why the individuals I have in mind would want to help me take care of my unfinished business. The first reason that, while they may not have thought about it in the way that I have, most people in the late stages of their careers or in the early months of retirement realize they have not accomplished some of their most cherished aspirations in life at this point and that they still would like to pursue these aspirations. There is a second group of talented and enterprising people who I know are interested in working on some of the projects that are embedded in my repertoire of unfinished professional and social business but for whom time is money because of their current professional and family obligations. Some of these folks, my former colleagues and friends, would welcome the opportunity to collaborate with me on our respective agendas of unfinished business relative to educational change, renewal, innovation, community development, student academic and enrichment programs, parental support, and other projects that might be extracted from my mines of unfinished business. Therefore When I contemplate the promise and potential of such altruistic collaboration, I experience *"gusts"* of creativity, excitement, and anticipation that boost and elevate my gusto. On a directly personal note, **my gusto really soars** when I imagine how I can involve my husband, Malcolm, our sons, friends, and former colleagues and coworkers in my unfinished business projects that focus on helping students and parents, improving schools, universities, and communities.

Tackling the unfinished business from my professional years is not something I am just musing about. I am doing something about my unfinished business by creating two organizations that will make an effective attack on my unfinished business possible. The first step I took was to establish the **Beacon of Hope Foundation**. The purpose of the Beacon of Hope Foundation is to raise funds for the support of scholarships and other worthwhile projects in a variety of nonprofit educational and community ventures. The second and most recently step I have taken is to establish a for-profit entity, **CIS Education Consulting, LLC**. The purpose of CSI Education Consulting is to provide coordinated services for the improvement of education in schools, colleges, universities and communities. I am pleased to observe that my family, friends, and former colleagues are actively supporting each of these ventures. I am hopeful that each will grow in their capacity and effectiveness in helping me address some of the opportunities to benefit my fellow citizens through endeavors inspired by my unfinished business.

At this point, I would like to describe some of the items of unfinished business to which I am referring. I would like to select a few examples from each of my career plateaus. Early in my teaching career I was recognized by my mentor and supervisor, Mr. Matthew H. Estaras, as a strong and effective teacher who had the potential to become a good administrator. Over the course of my career as a high school teacher, I learned how to challenge and motivate my students. I set high expectations for my students and demanded high quality class work from them. During those years I augmented my teaching experiences with advanced study in teacher education and educational administration; as a result I acquired knowledge, skills, and dispositions that made me a highly effective teacher and administrator. However, time commitment, school structures and operations did not allow me to coach and mentor other teachers and administrators, especially new teachers and administrators, who joined the faculty or administration each year during my tenure. In order to address this item of unfinished business, I am committed now to coaching and mentoring new teachers and educational leaders through professional development programs offered by my firm, CSI Education Consulting. On the first plateau of my career, I conceived and founded the **_Martin Luther King Jr., Service and Scholarship Society (MLKSSS)_** for high school students at the FAMU Developmental Research School. The MLKSS Society promoted giving service to worthy causes, fostered high self-esteem, good citizenship and scholarship on the part of FAMU DRS students. It has been inactive for some years. I would like to explore the feasibility of reactivating that organization and spreading it to other schools throughout this state. While on the second plateau of my professional career, I developed the **Head Start to High School Summer Program**, a summer transition program for rising ninth graders. It is my intention to restart and reinvigorate this program because it showed great promise for helping student transitioning from middle school to high school with high levels of academic success in ninth grade. During my tenure as Director of the FAMU Center for Teacher Preparation and Director of the Evening and Weekend College, I led the development of programs that promoted the retention of students and enhanced their academic staying power, contributed to the increased production of teachers by the College of Education. While on the third plateau of my career, one of the special programs I developed was the personal finance module for the Freshman Orientation Course. The intent of this course was to help entering freshman avoid the credit traps that resulted from the abuse of readily available credit cards to students who were essentially unemployed or under employed. The senior administrative plateau gave me many opportunities to expand my knowledge of virtually every aspect of university operations and sharpened my management skills. Some of the problems and challenges facing FAMU when I was in senior administration as a Dean and later as Interim Provost still confront other college and university administrators. It is through my consulting firm, CIS Education Consulting, that I plan to assist colleges and universities in addressing problems and challenges in the area of student retention and graduation rates, increasing the production of highly qualified teacher education graduates, grant writing and project evaluation, to name a few.

I believe that I have much in common and much to share with professional women who are nearing retirement or who have recently retired as it relates to finding the gusto related to the unfinished business, unfulfilled aspirations and undeveloped talents we can give our attention to in the early retirement years. We should hardly be surprised that we are creative, talented, resourceful, industrious, wise, confident, smart, and ingenious individuals possessing a unique, rich and diverse body of experiences which should be a well spring for the gusto and excitement about the opportunity that retirement gives us to redesign our lives for the better and to refocus our energies and gifts, both secular and spiritual, in ways of our own choosing to shape our futures.

When a woman retires from fulltime employment in her career, she has many options, not just addressing unfinished business as I am doing, for continuing to be an active and productive member of society and most of all retaining her "gusto". These post-career opportunities for productive activities could be categorized in the following way in addition to other categories as follows:

- Participation/leadership in professional organizations with the objective of helping prepare the next generation of professionals in her field. For example, serving as preceptors or competition judges, etc.
- Going from professional practice to teaching or research. For example, a lawyer or judge could join the faculty of a law school after retiring from a law firm or retiring from the bench.
- A woman having grandchildren could spend part of her time developing the talents of her grandchildren through the facilitation of their participation in schools activities, summer

programs and social organizations such as Jack and Jill of America, Inc.

- A woman could retire from any field and get involved part-time in advocacy for causes that she has been interested in for a long time but career commitments would not allow her to pursue. There are many advocacy groups committed to many causes such as the Doctors without Borders, the NAACP, Common Cause, church related organizations, and the national programs of service clubs and sororities.

- A woman whose career did not serve as an outlet for her creative and artistic talents could engage herself in the development or expression of her talents through such activities as creative writing, musicianship, painting, crafts, etc.

- A woman who is inclined to do so could attempt to take talents that she possesses and develop them into a profitable business, for example a **"good"** cook could start a restaurant or prepare and sell her special cakes, pie, jellies, or barbeque sauces. The internet has made such endeavors feasible and profitable for some women.

These categories of post-career opportunities could be expanded to include other options including starting a new career in a specialty area of her previous career, for example, a family physician could pursue pediatrics as a second career, or launch a second career in an area unrelated to the first career, for example, a science teacher could become a farmer. Other examples of post retirement transformations are:

From Classroom Teacher to Executive University Management and Administration to Entrepreneur and Non-profit President, the Dr. Barbara K. Barnes' Example

- **From Teacher to Performing Artist, the Dr. Mary Roberts' Example**
- **From Classroom Teacher to the School Board Chair, the Maggie Lewis' Example**
- **From Business Education Teacher to Entrepreneur and Champion of the Homeless, the Dr. Carolyn Johnson Ryals' Example**
- **From Associate Vice President to Church Leader, the Dr. Eva C. Wanton Example**
- **From University Administrator to Realtor, the Dr. Clinita Ford Example**
- **From News Anchor to TV personality to Philanthropist Extraordinaire, the Oprah Winfrey Example**

My emphasis up to this point has primarily focused on the secular approaches to maintaining a woman's gusto after retirement. Now, I would like to briefly discuss some of the spiritual aspects of maintaining one's gusto, not just after retirement but throughout ones adult life.

While a woman's recognition after retirement of unfinished business, her unfulfilled aspirations, her undeveloped talents, uncommitted gifts or even her discovery of a new purpose for her life, new business, might ignite gusto, I am convinced that these realizations cannot sustain gusto. On a personal note, I was recognized by the Capital Outlook newspaper of Tallahassee, Florida on January 28, 2010 as one of the Top Twenty-five Leaders in Tallahassee. While this recognition of my career and service contributions have elevated my gusto, this elevation will probably be short-term. This is most likely to be true because I believe that only a woman's heart filled with thanksgiving can sustain gusto. By the time a woman reaches the stage of life when she retires, she has certainly encountered and overcome many problems, hurdles, and challenges. She has likely overcome health challenges, financial challenges, and even spiritual challenges. If she has children, either as a single parent or with the help of her partner, she has faced the challenges of rearing children and possibly even rearing grandchildren. For me personally, when I look back over my life, I see stumbling blocks turned into stepping-stones. I see challenges turned into opportunities. I do not believe that neither these nor other vicissitudes of my life were accidents or chance occurrences. But, I think that they were all a part of God's plan for my life. I read in Jeremiah 29:11 "For I know the plans I have for you," declares the LORD, "plans to prosper you and not to harm you, plans to give you hope and a future. I am grateful for what God's plan for my life has revealed from the beginning of my career up to and beyond retirement. Because I believe that the Lord plans to prosper me in my retirement as He has in my career. Because I have this God given hope, "spiritual gusto", I eagerly face each day for its revelation of what God's plan for my future is.

As a Christian woman, my heart is joyful when I think how blessed I am to have reached the stage of my life where I can start my day with Christian meditation giving thanks to God for the many blessing He bestowed upon me throughout my life. When I realized that I have the health, strength, and desire to be of service to people in need, I conclude that my life has the dual purpose of service and testimony.

I will serve others primarily through my gifts as an educator with unfinished business, because I agree completely with President Barack Obama, who said "The best anti-poverty program is a quality education." In addition, I will encourage women, especially stressed, challenged and troubled women, whom I meet through my personal story and through words from the Bible. Each day I will encourage myself with the thought that ***"This is the day that the Lord has made, we will rejoice and be glad in it."*** (Psalm 118:24). I am convinced that the gusto that I need to thrive as retired woman will be ignited by my desired to tackle some of my unfinished business, and I am also convinced that this gusto will be fueled by my spirit of gratitude and joy that I have another day to serve God by serving others. Psalm 118:24 states, "we will rejoice and be glad in it." This implies the **"we"** can choose to rejoice and can choose to be glad. Consequently, I believe that we can choose to keep our gusto as opposed to letting it depart from us. I make this claim because I believe that gusto is one part joy, one part gladness, and one part purpose. Recall that our scripture states that we will be glad in it, ***the day.*** To me this means that there is something that I will do or experience during the day that will make me glad. That something is the purpose of that day. If the day is a day that I spend attending to "unfinished business," then I will be glad in it. If today is a day of meditation and worship, then I will be glad it also. By rejoicing and being glad that we have another day to pursue the purpose that we have chosen for this day, we are endowed with gusto for this day. If we, the contributors to this book and those persons in our respective spheres of influence, would let Psalm 118:24 be manifested in our lives on a daily or even weekly basis and if we will endeavor to **"find faith in everything that we do,"** then, our lives and the lives of many we touch will be filled with gladness, joy, and gusto.

Achieving Gusto through Navigating Broad Career Experiences

Marjorie Turnbull

At the age of 60, I walked a marathon. It was 26.2 miles of windy, drizzling, 33 degree weather in Dublin, Ireland. The physical challenge, the learning experience, the enjoyment of camaraderie and the cause, raising money for a non-profit organization, all contributed to the euphoria I felt when I crossed the finish line. It was a bellwether for my retirement six years later.

For me, retirement was not rushing away from anything. I worked with wonderful people, regularly engaged in new ideas and experiences and felt privileged to have the job I had. In fact throughout my years of employment, I had only one job that made me grit my teeth when I arose in the morning--the one that taught me the most.

Prior to retirement, I confess to being over-engaged, a hyper multi-tasker who took pride in a full calendar. When a meeting was cancelled or there was an unexpected calendar glitch, I was antsy at having unplanned time. I juggled three "to do" lists – personal, work and community service.

For 12 years I served in elected office, first on the Leon County Commission and subsequently in the Florida Legislature. To say my life during this time belonged to the people is an understatement. Constituents felt free, as they should, to call my home at any time or stop me at the grocery store or other venues to discuss one issue or another. After two years in office, my aide finally trained me not to make commitments without my calendar (and her oversight!). While on the county commission, I was additionally employed as a lobbyist for non-profit agencies. As a Legislator, I held a full-time job at the community college. Fitting all these tasks into a day required great creativity and resulted in little sleep.

This recitation of work and public service is to provide a base for understanding how I approached and planned for retirement.

I felt fairly confident that boredom would not be an issue, having failed to be bored since long summers as a child. Nonetheless, it was clear that major adjustments would occur in the future. Two potential adjustments loomed: First, how to redefine myself and second, how to fill the hours in the day.

Let me digress and share with you that there was one other time in my life when I had to redefine myself and that was when my husband of 26 years died of cancer. He had been my biggest booster and fan. He was the one who said "do it" when I resisted the encouragement of others to run for public office. Since we did not have children, we combined two high energy careers into one shared and interesting life. No paycheck, public office, or community recognition filled the void he provided to understanding who I was. It was this past struggle with redefinition that lent confidence to the task of redefinition in retirement.

Work does define us. When someone asks, "What are you doing now?" as people inevitably do, we are quick to describe the job we hold if employed. This information opens up many avenues for conversation. But when you are retired, and answer the question with "I'm retired," either the conversation stops or two inevitable questions follow: First, "Are you traveling?" and second, "Are you planning to stay here?" For me these were conversation non-starters since traveling had always been part of my life rather than something saved for retirement, and it never occurred to me to live anywhere but "here,"

It became clear that redefining oneself, other than as a member of the work force, required moving away from the strongly held concept that one's value is in a paycheck or the accomplishment of employment goals.

Another major adjustment was admitting the distinct possibility that the phone would stop ringing, no one would call for lunch and what used to be a blank hour on the calendar might turn into weeks. Before retirement, there was always more to do than time available. So I faced accepting the fact that I would not be expected at the next meeting or, even more difficult, that I would be completely in charge of my time.

It became clear that retirement was not something I could do suddenly. As anyone in a managerial or leadership position knows, there are good reasons for strategic planning. Therefore, I made the decision to retire one year before the actual date and seven months before I announced it to anyone else. This strategy gave me time to plan without interference.

My planning process was not very sophisticated. Step one meant conversations I had with myself. They went something like this: Face it – you may fade into the woodwork, you may have to search for ways to keep occupied, it is quite possible no one will remember you. Or the alternative optimistic scenario – this is going to be the best time of your life, put aside your fears and start making lists of all those things you have always wanted to do, all the adventures in learning you missed, all the good causes you were unable to help, all the family and friends you have neglected.

Step two were conversations I had with friends who had retired. When the response to the question of "How are you enjoying retirement?" was unenthusiastic or even hesitant, they were struck from my research list. But when the response was, "It is wonderful, the best thing that ever happened to me," I suggested we have lunch.

I wish I had kept notes from these conversations. A sociologist would have recorded and analyzed the common threads among those who were relishing their retirement. A rough collation of their thoughts boils down to the following: First, they seemed to agree that retirement was not an ending or even a beginning but an encore. It was seen as an opportunity to excel further and achieve a higher level of performance because this part of life was built on a solid foundation of learning and accomplishment. Second, invariably they noted that "retirement" was placed in quotes. They were busier than ever. Some continued to work part time, no longer needing title or salary size to motivate them. But the filling of the hours was not based on stressful demands either from above or below but rather on conscious decisions of what would bring enjoyment to themselves and others.

Something else stood out –giving back. Happy retirees see themselves as having the time they didn't have as younger folks with families and jobs to volunteer in significant and useful ways.

Some of those who were happiest in retirement took off on entirely new roads – a former association manager became involved in acting in films and writing plays, a former university administrator took up jewelry making, a former minister became a math tutor. Others took volunteer paths connected to their earlier employment. A historian volunteered at the state archives, a librarian helped children learn to read, a professor taught slow learners.

With this knowledge, I began to explore future activities or commitments. I am not overly adventuresome. I tend to be a nester, having lived in the same town for 36 years and the same house for 33. Predictability and continuity hold a certain amount of comfort. I like the chocolate boxes with the lids that tell you what each piece is. I travel around the world knowing that home awaits me.

My *bucket list* does include such things as going on an African safari and attending a NASCAR race, the Academy Awards, the Kentucky Derby, and one of the last Shuttle liftoffs. But although these activities will be new experiences, they are decidedly within my comfort zone. It would have been a total waste of time putting such things as skydiving or bunji cord jumping on the list.

The first fear after retirement that proved unfounded – that the phone would stop ringing – forced me to adopt a set of "rules" in accepting suggestions from those who wanted to include me in their favorite projects. I decided I would make no commitments for a year. (Warning: People write these things down and call you back when the year is up!)

Second, three criteria –that came together in the Dublin marathon – would direct my choices for taking on new challenges. 1) Would it be a learning experience? 2) Would it help other people? 3) Would it be enjoyable and even fun? It was refreshing to have guidelines that allowed me to say "no" without guilt and move forward with gusto.

What has captured my "yes?" I found I have stayed close to endeavors that extend my employment skills and experience. I serve on boards of three statewide foundations where my experience as a former foundation director has been useful. I am chairing a capital campaign, using my fund raising knowledge for a hospice program that gave support and comfort as my husband and I journeyed through his ordeal with cancer. I serve on the board of a program that encourages children to enter the critical fields of math and science. I have provided training in board development and fund raising for nonprofits to meet critical needs in tough economic times. Most recently, I have been appointed to a Board of Trustees of a state university.

Admittedly I am back to keeping a "to do" list after saying "yes" too many times. There are just so many good causes that meet the three rules and add exuberance to life.

But despite a full calendar, amazingly there is no stress. In retirement, stress is when my computer goes down or my "smart phone" (now there is an oxymoron if there ever was one) crashes. Stress means resenting the intrusion and control that the constant presence of e-mail and cell phone impose. (Is this the same person who feared the phone would stop ringing?)

Lest I leave the impression I've fully adjusted to retirement, let me admit that I still feel less guilty reading a good book on the weekend than on a weekday. I still have to catch myself from explaining to someone why I am shopping in the middle of the day rather than working at the office. I occasionally feel the need to answer the question "what are you doing now" with a description of some meaningful economically valued task.

Perhaps the most enriching part of retirement is being able to spend more time with family and friends. Obligations at work no longer dictate my schedule. The true spice in life is making the dress that my grandniece wore as flower girl in my niece's wedding, taking a week in the fall to tour Western national parks with my sister and brother-in-law or attending the Georgia State Fair to cheer my grandnephew as he presented his prize pig. From the perspective of retirement, regret is not having failed to spend more time on the job, but in failing to make extra time with family and friends.

My father, my life-long mentor, understood this. A busy man of great vigor, he loved people and engaged with enthusiasm every life phase, including retirement. He was once asked by a geriatrician at the University of Florida College of Medicine how he maintained a high level of vigor, interest and activity in life. His response worth sharing helped shaped my philosophy toward retirement:

1. Have a wife (husband) to love and adore, who looks after your welfare and provides a home

of peace and beauty. Keep close to your children even though they are no longer at home.

2. Arise regularly and take more than a mile walk before breakfast, preferably each day, but at least four times per week. A great time to do this is near sunrise when the birds are singing.

3. Have more to do each day than you can get done.

4. Be active in a church even if you cannot support totally its theology.

5. The things you do should involve goals and the support of causes which cannot be achieved in a lifetime as well as assistance to and concern for community needs, friends and others.

6. Save some time to work in the garden because the companion of plants has much to offer.

7. Read widely, enjoy good music, keep abreast of national and international affairs, and do not spend too much time with the TV.

8. View life positively and look for the good in people rather than their limitations.

9. Cherish and enjoy the company of friends

10. Follow a balanced diet and be ever moderate in eating and drinking.

11. Maintain a sense of humor.

12. Take a modest amount of time to enjoy outdoor recreation.

Let me conclude with the recognition that much of my ability to enjoy retirement is that I am in good health. Should the alternative occur, I have health insurance and a reasonable income that will still allow me choices. The decisions I made and the directions I took would be far more complicated and demanding if this were not so.

A retired friend who sits daily by the bedside of his gravely ill wife brightens the lives of others through e-mails worth saving because they are full of humor and beauty. His joy reinforces my conviction that gusto in retirement is a choice we make for ourselves.

Achieving Real Gusto through Membership and Participation in Civic and Social Organizations

Fanchon Felice Funk – "Fancy"

Connectedness
Social connectedness is one of the most important predictors of health and independence in later years.

> G. Richard Ambrosius, Author of Choices and Changes[1]

When I look back over my life's journey, I see how my love of learning and teaching has helped me build connections that have given my life gusto! Well, the journey doesn't end with retirement, and I was determined that my "life after work" would be fun, people-involved and meaningful. I knew that my involvement in social and civic associations was an answer for this part of my life journey.

As I share some of my life's story with you, I hope you may get some ideas that will help you reflect on your own life and see how what you have loved and accomplished can lay the foundation for a joyful future. I like what Connie Goldman said about life-learning in the dedication of her book on conversations with women in mid-life and the years beyond: "there are life lessons to be learned from others as well as from inside your very self."[2]

You may have read some of the research that says that people with strong relationships remain more vital both mentally and physically in the later years.[3] Research also reveals that one of our basic needs is to belong, to be part of something beyond and greater than ourselves. That has certainly been true for me and is even more so now in my retirement.

My connections begin with the love of my family (my sister, four nieces and nephews, nine grand nieces and nephews, one great grand-niece, and my godson). These important connections continue to my extended families through spiritual, civic and social organizations. These are the connections that give my life real gusto. There is a saying associated with my birth city of New Orleans that, to me, literally shouts GUSTO in life:
L'aissez, les bons temps rouler! The translation for this is "Let the good times roll!"

By the way, my connection to New Orleans provides the answer to a question I am frequently asked: Where in the world did your nickname come from? One answer is that "Fancy" is a name that goes back before the Civil War. A Louisiana family named their daughter that because an older child looked at her new baby sister who had bright red hair and declared, 'She's not like our other baby, she's more fancy. Every other generation now has a "Fancy." A simpler explanation for my name is that "Fancy" is short for Fanchon, which was difficult to spell and pronounce.

Now, back to my pursuit of gusto. Since I officially retired January 31, 2004 after 34 years of employment as a faculty member in the College of Education, Florida State University (FSU), I have been involved in a number of civic and social organizations. I found, as you may also, that my past interests, connections, and experiences have formed a basis for this exciting new stage in my life. Thinking back over how I got to where I am now, I see several common themes that intertwine to make my life today rich and rewarding.

Get Active and Stay Active

By now you know that in order to enjoy life, you must work to stay healthy by exercising both mind and body. My favorite physical exercise is swimming, but I also enjoy a good workout at the gym. To exercise my mind, I enjoy reading and travel. While these things help to keep me fit, they are not enough to maintain that vitality that brings gusto to life. My joy comes from working with people by networking and opening doors for others—in other words, making connections. Many folks have done this for me, and I've got a lot of giving back to do!

My life of being connected didn't end when I retired, and it didn't begin there, either. What I do now is a continuation of civic and social activities that began in the early days of my career. I have always been involved in education. In 1958, I began teaching biology, chemistry, and physics at Lee Edwards High School in Asheville, N.C. I also joined the Asheville Classroom Teachers' Association (CTA). Two years later, the President of this organization inspired and encouraged me to follow in her footsteps to participate in the Fulbright Teacher Exchange Program. I was serving on the Board of the CTA in 1961 when I learned that my application to the Fulbright Program had been accepted. I taught science in Ilford, Essex, England in 1962-1963. While in Europe, I participated in personal seminars for Comparative Education Studies, visiting schools of all levels in nineteen countries. I don't believe I would have had this incredible experience had I not become involved in the CTA and made the connection with the President who encouraged me.

Well, by this time I was in love with education. Not being satisfied with two Bachelor of Science degrees in biology and education (Western Carolina University), I completed a Masters in Arts degree in biology and junior college instruction (Appalachian State University). I next earned my Doctoral Degree in Curriculum and Instruction, with collateral areas in Higher Education and Public Health (University of Tennessee, Knoxville) in 1970.

I began my career at FSU in August, 1970, as an area coordinator of student teaching/field experiences. Six years later I became Director of the Office of Clinical Education and was promoted to associate professor with tenure in the Department of Educational Leadership & Policy Studies. If I were a less active person, I might have been satisfied to limit my service to that position, but there was more I wanted to give, and each new opportunity for service created new connections to the future.

Other administrative positions that I held with the University were: Director of Inter-Institutional Relations, Associate Director of the Center for Performance Technology, and Customer Satisfaction Researcher for the Schoolyear 2000 Initiative. While these positions helped me to develop professionally, it was my direct involvement with students that helped me satisfy some of my desire to give back. For example, I served as Instructor in the innovative First Year Experience Program for entering freshmen at FSU and as a Mentor for the University Genesis Program for outstanding freshmen students who were destined to become future leaders of the university. I rounded out my career at FSU by serving as Director of the Office of Alumni Affairs in the Dean's Office, College of Education (COE). Interacting with COE graduates throughout the world was a fantastic experience. As they shared their accomplishments, I could see the continuation of growth that began at FSU.

There are many other opportunities to maintain connections and activities that are begun during one's career days. For me, these include being active in my Church, The Delta Kappa Gamma Society International, the Order of the Eastern Star, the Rebekah Lodge, Omicron Delta Kappa Honorary, Phi Kappa Phi Honorary, Kappa Delta Pi International Honorary Society in Education, the Mortar Board National College Honor Society, the University Center Club, and the Capital Women's Network.

"Every job is a reflection of the person who did it
– autograph your work with excellence"

I believe so strongly in this quote that I use it in the signature line of my email address. I also can relate this quote to something John Barrymore said: "Happiness often sneaks through a door you didn't know you left open." Doing your very best in all that you do can open doors for you to pursue what interests you most. Sometimes pursuing excellence provides opportunities you never dream will appear. Here is one I never expected: During my participation in the Fulbright Teacher Exchange, I was deeply honored to have been selected by Her Majesty's Minister for Education for the Official Presentation to Her Royal Highness Elizabeth, the Queen Mother, on behalf of American Fulbright Teacher Exchanges (79 in England and 421 in other countries) at a Formal Reception in London in July, 1963.

In my early years as an educator, I was pleased to be selected to participate in two National Science Foundation programs for science teachers, one in 1960 and the other in 1966. I learned that taking time to participate in such activities can provide opportunities to meet many new people who share common interests. I still take advantage of opportunities today that allow me to meet new people and grow.

Another experience that I will never forget was the ten years I served as the Facilitator and Coordinator for the world wide Walt Disney World Educator Seminars, offered for academic credit through FSU. During this time, over 14,000 educators from every state in the nation and 38 countries joined us at Disney World to participate at what I refer to as the greatest experiential learning laboratory in the world. Would I have been selected for this honor if I had never been as active and involved as I was in my career to this point?

I also discovered that excellence in community service can be rewarded as well as rewarding. The DELTA Alumni Chapter of Phi Theta Kappa (PTK) is the Honorary of the Community Colleges, and its bright undergraduate students are high achievers dedicated to both their academic studies and community service. Community service activities included serving meals at The Shelter for the Homeless. I was delighted to serve as Advisor for the FSU chapter of PTK and must brag a little about these special students. The chapter began in 1984 with three students and by 1992 had grown to over 50 students per year. During this time, the chapter won every award available at the state and national levels! I still hear from several of these exceptional students and rejoice in their amazing accomplishments.

I feel very blessed to have been recognized for my efforts in teacher education, not only during my career, but in the year of my retirement. In 2004, I received the Roy L. Lauter Distinguished Service Award from the Southeastern Regional Association of Teacher Educators, the highest member recognition by this extremely active regional association. Also in 2004, I received the Association of Teacher Educators Distinguished Member Award, the highest recognition of a member at the national level.

Keep Expanding Your Connections

I continue many of the activities I began during my professional career. One of these is supporting education and building a family connection to community and future generations. In 2008, I was elected an Honorary Member of the Kirksville College of Osteopathic Medicine Alumni Association and was presented with the Distinguished Patron Award of the American Osteopathic Association (AOA). As the daughter and granddaughter of Osteopathic Physicians, I feel certain that my early career goal of becoming an osteopathic physician would have been a reality had I not fallen in love with the profession of education.

When presented with the patron award by the National AOA President, I shared the following: "I support the scholarship program at the Kirksville College of Osteopathic Medicine in memory of my father and grandfather, who were the first father and son to graduate in the same year from KCOM. That year was 1931 (records indicate this has not happened since). I know that through such gifts, future generations of medical students will receive the same outstanding training in osteopathic medicine that my father and grandfather received. Each year it is an honor to receive the thank you notes from the student doctors who have received these scholarships. My family and I celebrate these young doctors whose education we have been able to support. I am deeply honored."

My connection with education and the future also continues through FSU. During my professional career, I was fortunate to have been the recipient of several outstanding teaching awards and recognitions. However, the most amazing and gratifying event occurred at my retirement reception on January 29, 2004, when it was announced that my students, family, colleagues, and friends had established an endowed scholarship in my name! Each year, undergraduate and graduate teacher education majors in the FSU College of Education will enjoy financial benefits from this scholarship. This is absolutely thrilling and at the same time extremely humbling.

Philanthropy has become a passion in my retirement. Throughout my life people have made such comments to me as . . . *bet you've never met a stranger*. True! I enjoy meeting people and learning about the uniqueness of each one. In 2008, a new and active group was formed at FSU: The Women for Florida State University. A similar group was formed ten years ago at my alma mater, the University of Tennessee, the Alliance of Women Philanthropists. These women are on the move. Most have reached that energized state in life called retirement. Fund raising and remaining connected to one's institution (whether by degree or adopted by employment) is absolutely invigorating!

My involvement with scholarships and fundraising for Florida universities did not begin when I retired. From 1986 until the present, I have been a member and Chair of the Board of Directors (1999-2000) of the Southern Scholarship Foundation (SSF). The SSF is a non-profit organization that provides rent free housing for over 415 students living in 25 scholarship houses located near four Florida University campuses. I am now delighted to bring the perspective of a retiree to this Board. My fund raising learning curve has definitely taken an energized leap forward for SSF. This is a wonderful way for retiree associations of all kinds to become mentors and provide support to assist young students in obtaining their degrees.

Some fundraising activities are great fun— such as being a docent. For the past four years I have enjoyed meeting hundreds of dedicated members of the Tallahassee Symphony Society by serving as a docent for the annual Holiday Tour of Homes, which is a fundraiser for the Symphony. I am also one of fifteen members of the FSU Association of Retired Faculty and Staff (ARF—don't laugh!) who have volunteered to serve as docents for the FSU's President's House since its opening August

2007. We have the opportunity of welcoming thousands of guests and visitors to this beautiful house and sharing their excitement for this part of the University's history.

There are other valuable associations in which to become active. In August 2008, ARF joined the prestigious International Association of Retirement Organizations in Higher Education (AROHE). At the 2008 International Conference held at the University of Southern California, I was pleased to be elected to the AROHE Board of Directors. Presently, as Chair of International Regional Conferences for AROHE, I am engaged in planning the first Regional which will be a Conference-at-Sea for Retirement Organizations in Higher Education in North America, April 2011.

For a change of pace, I enjoy serving on the Executive Board of Directors of the Character & Heritage Institute, a non-profit multi-media company which provides education through the arts. It is exciting to work with young people and educators and observe the DVD "movie" they produce in three weeks. This program, *Operation Filmmaker*, is presently focused on Middle and High School students with plans to move production to the lower grades as well. Participants quickly learn that this program is about more than making a movie.

Another change of pace, and a return to my early interest in biology and science, is my involvement with The Regal Swan® Foundation, Inc. As a member of the Board of Directors and Vice President, I write articles for professional journals and have co-authored several books, including the *SWAN KEEPER'S HANDBOOK: A Guide to the Care of Captive Swans*. The Regal Swan® Foundation,

Inc. is a research team based in Orlando, Florida. The team is composed of professionals from a variety of avian and medical disciplines worldwide and is committed to the humane veterinary medical care of swans.

Collaborating with Her Majesty's Swan Warden, Dr. Christopher Perrins (London, England), nine of the 31 worldwide members of the research team were invited to England in the summer of 2007 to conduct research concerning the pink flamingo (pink feathers) syndrome. The medical care and feeding of the English Mute Swan is our specialty, and I found it fascinating to have the unique opportunity of being part of the British research agenda for swans. In addition, being part of the annual Swan Upping in England is one of those experiences that is unforgettable. A Swan Upping is a practice that began in medieval times when the English Crown claimed ownership of all mute swans and involves the capture, counting, marking and physical examination of the swans. Historically, The Queen's Swan Warden, whose role is scientific and non-ceremonial, rings cygnets with individual identifications numbers.

Research team members have given presentations to education and scientific groups, universities, zoos and museums, Florida pK-12 teachers, community organizations, and numerous professional associations. We have a passion for our work. In fact, being passionate about what you do is a key to living with Gusto!

Going for the Gusto

The GUSTO in retirement has captured my heart, and I want to be among people who enjoy life as much as I do. In 2006, I became a founding member of the Westcott Lakes Life Fulfilling Community, a.k.a., the *Pavilion* at Westcott Lakes. Knowing that this community would be sponsored by FSU really captivated me. What a win-win partnership! The academic and cultural opportunities provided by Florida State University will be numerous and exceptional. It will be great fun to have wonderful friends as neighbors in a lifelong learning environment.

I know that by now you must be saying to yourself—but I thought she was *retired*! Well, life is just too much fun not to stay involved and connected. I like a quote by Peter Drucker in a research study on aging and civic engagement: "The best way to predict the future is to create it."[5] We can create a positive future by enjoying life, friends, family, extended family, and involvement in and through religious, civic, and professional engagements. And if life so far has limited your opportunities to connect and get involved, it's not too late to start to create a future that will bring *you* gusto!

I began this chapter with a quotation from G. R. Ambrosius, and I will end it with another of his wise sayings: "By mindfully pursuing positive aging, later life may come to be perceived as the crown jewel of the human experience."[6] Yes indeed, as we say in New Orleans, *let the good times roll!* The best is yet to come.

Footnotes

1. Ambrosius, G. Richard, Choices and Changes: A Positive Aging Guide to Life Planning, Xlibris Corporation, 2006.

2. Goldman, Connie. Who Am I...Now That I'm Not Who I was? Conversations with women in mid-life and the years beyond. 2009.

3. AARP and the Dana Alliance for Brain Initiatives, Current Advance in Brain Research, "Staying Sharp – Quality of Life, Washington, D.C.,
2005, p.97.

4. Schwartz, Marilyn. A Southern Belle Primer. 2001. p.9.

5. Civic Ventures and Temple University Center for International Learning, *Recasting Retirement: New Perspectives on Aging and Civic Engagement* (2002).The publication highlights the findings and was sponsored by a grant from the Helen Andrus Benedict Foundation.

6. Ambrosius, 2006. p.120.

Real Gusto Comes Later: An Integrative Perspective

Lorraine T. Dorfman

Retirement, one of the major role transitions of later life, signifies for most people formal separation from the paid labor force and entry into a new stage of life. This means, among other things, a realignment of how time is spent, and for many people, decisions about how to spend that time in personally meaningful and fulfilling pursuits. Retirement thus represents a challenge as well as an opportunity for the individual that may call for some personal reinvention. Most retirees develop a new and satisfying life structure and pattern of activities after their initial adjustment to this new life stage, especially if their retirement was voluntary, planned and anticipated.

This chapter begins by reviewing several major theoretical perspectives that are relevant to retirement and aging and gives illustrations with examples drawn from the case studies and life histories provided by the "gusto women" represented in this book. The chapter goes on to discuss major empirical findings concerning the relationship between activity and psychosocial well-being in retirement, again using materials provided by the gusto women to illustrate. In some cases, direct quotations from the women are used in order to give voice to the thoughts and experiences of this remarkable group of professional women.

Theoretical Perspectives

Early work in social gerontology provided two contrasting theoretical perspectives on activity and adaptation in later life: activity theory (Havighurst & Albrecht, 1953; Lemon, Bengston, & Peterson, 1972) and disengagement theory (Cumming & Henry, 1961). According to activity theory, in order to age successfully retired people need to maintain high activity levels, which in turn contribute to social integration and life satisfaction (Havighurst & Albrecht, 1953). Essentially, activity theory posits a positive relationship between activity and late-life satisfaction and suggests that the greater the role loss, the lower the satisfaction (Lemon et al., 1972). Consequently, continued activity, preferably from the levels of middle age, is the route to satisfaction and to the person's sense of identity and continued participation in social roles (McGuire, Boyd, & Tedrick, 2009), and lost roles need to be replaced with new ones. Activity participation can include informal activities such as visiting with and/or helping family, friends and neighbors, formal participation as a volunteer or in clubs or other organizations, or solitary activities such as reading, watching television, or hobbies engaged in alone. Disengagement theory, in contrast to activity theory, holds that it is adaptive for older people to withdraw from work and other social roles in order to age successfully (Cumming & Henry, 1961). Furthermore, this relationship is seen as reciprocal, with society also withdrawing social roles from the older individual as she or he ages. Applied to retirement, disengagement theory suggests that it is functional for the older person to withdraw from work and for society to facilitate withdrawal from the labor force. The preponderance of evidence, however, supports an activity rather than a disengagement perspective on aging. For example, Rowe and Kahn (1997) in summarizing the long term, multidisciplinary MacArthur studies of successful aging, found successful aging to be characterized by active engagement in life in addition to the absence of disease and good physical and cognitive function. Furthermore, Nimrod's (2008) data revealed that adding new leisure activities after retirement contributes to well-being among recent retirees. Indeed, there may be some self-reinvention in retirement with retirees behaving in new and different ways (Nimrod & Kleiber, 2007). Some of the gusto women in this book exemplified the pattern of taking on new activities in retirement, as illustrated by the case of the physician who became a licensed realtor and who also took up painting after retiring. Another gusto woman embarked on and completed a Ph.D. degree and now serves as a consultant, is involved in national educational organizations, and travels a great deal with educator groups. A third woman learned to play the cello in retirement. This movement in new directions, sometimes involving self-reinvention, may occur as individuals age even before the actual event of retirement, as happened to one of the gusto women who had been a high-functioning dean at a major research university. That woman decided to step down from "deaning" after spending a considerable number of years in that role and found an entirely new direction by establishing a successful center aimed at improving the health and lives of underserved populations through research and program development.

One interesting theoretical perspective that in some ways relates to activity is the model of selective optimization with compensation (Baltes & Baltes, 1990; Baltes & Cartensen, 1996). Elements of this model include *selection*, in which the older individual concentrates on few domains that have a high priority, *optimization*, in which the individual engages in certain behaviors or activities that enrich their lives, and *compensation*, where certain behavioral capacities are lost and are compensated with by other perhaps less strenuous or demanding, activities. This theoretical perspective may help explain how people adjust their activity levels to decrements in health and energy as they grow older.

A theoretical perspective that has garnered considerable support in gerontology is continuity theory (Atchley, 1993, 1999, 2003). Continuity theory proposes that continuity of both ideas, values and personality ("internal continuity") and activities and lifestyle ("external continuity") are important in the continuing process of adult development in later life. According to Atchley (2003), the theory presumes that "most people continuously learn from their life experiences and intentionally continue to grow and evolve in different directions of their own choosing" (p. 125). Continuity is seen as a general pattern that allows for adaptive change to new circumstances as well as continuity of earlier ideas and behaviors; this in turn will contribute to life satisfaction of people as they age and their circumstances change. It is important to point out, however, that although change can and does occur in the continuity theory perspective, most people will prefer continuity to the extent that it is possible (Atchley, 1993). Many of the gusto women were exemplars of the basic tenets of continuity theory, with respect to both internal and external continuity. For example, two of the women wrote about the importance of continuing to have a positive attitude throughout life in overcoming adversity, thus illustrating consistency of one of their fundamental values (internal continuity). Likewise, many women illustrated external continuity in their behavior and lifestyle, such as the restaurateur who wrote of continuing her entrepreneurial activities in retirement by opening two new restaurants; she now operates a total of five restaurants. This woman also continued with her costume design activities for the Florida State University opera. Another gusto woman continued to participate in many social and civic organizations and boards that aim to serve others, as well as continuing travel related to her training in science (in particular, a specialty related to research on swans). That woman summarized all of her activities this way: "My joy comes from working with people by networking and opening doors for others – in other words, making connections. Many folks have done this for me, and I've got a lot of giving back to do!" In a different vein, a third gusto woman wrote of the importance of long-term financial planning and management of financial resources, which she had engaged in long before retirement and continued to follow carefully into her retirement years. Perhaps, however, the longest example of continuity over the life course was revealed in the words of a 92-year-old woman who spoke of continuing to "tickle the ivories," which meant her piano playing and her many related musical activities from age eight into advanced old age.

Related in some ways to continuity theory is the life course perspective, which is an adult development theory that helps to illuminate the retirement process. Some of the major concepts of life course theory are that human development is a lifelong process and that humans have agency to construct their life course within the historical and social context in which it occurs (Elder, Johnson, & Crosnoe, 2003). With respect to the first concept, the life course perspective posits that patterns of adaptation in later life are linked to earlier phases of development, and with respect to the second, the perspective purposes that individuals are not passively acted upon, but make choices based on the alternatives that they perceive are available to them (Elder et al., 2003). The gusto women almost without exception illustrated these two principles, with many describing their retirement experiences and choices in relation to earlier stages in their personal and professional development. In this way, they provided a glimpse for the reader of how their life course unfolded. Likewise, the women illustrated the principle of agency by vigorously acting upon the choices and alternatives that were available to them in retirement.

Activity and Well-Being in Retirement

Satisfaction in retirement is often associated with participation in activities that can replace the rewards that were obtained from pre-retirement work, including feelings of achievement, personal growth, desire for recognition and social interaction (Floyd, Haynes, Doll, Winemiller, Lansky, Burgy et al., 1992; Kelly, 1982). There is evidence also that life satisfaction is positively related not only to activity participation, but to frequency of that participation (Bevil, O'Connor, & Nattiib, 1999; Nimrod, 2007a; Sener, Terzioglu, & Karabulut, 2007). Indeed, some observers such as Peppers (1976) report that life satisfaction is highest among retirees who increase their number of activities. One caveat is that it may be unrealistic for all retirees to maintain a high activity level due to energy and/or health declines, or simply because once retired they may prefer to have a more relaxed lifestyle than formerly, free of many structured activities. It is also important to note that there is a reciprocal relationship between activity participation and psychological well-being; in other words, activity can be a cause or an effect of psychological well-being. Yet, as Cohen (2003) has pointed out, it may be helpful in later life to develop a "social portfolio" of activities and interpersonal relationships that can contribute to maintaining mental health. Perhaps, however, it is the *quality* and satisfaction with activity participation as much as participation itself that is important in assessing overall life satisfaction in retirement (Guinn, 1999; Litwin & Shiovitz, 2006; Sener et al., 2007).

The question then arises: What kinds of retirement activities tend to contribute to psychosocial well-being in retirement, especially for women? There is some evidence that gender differences do exist in both activity level and activity preferences of retired women and men (Freysinger, Alessio, & Mehdizadeh, 1993; Iwasaki & Smale, 1998), with women generally placing more emphasis on activities involving socializing than do men.

Research often identifies activities involving informal social interaction as being particularly important in the social and psychological adaptation of older people (Iwasaki & Smale, 1998; Menec, 2003; O'Brien, 1981; Peppers, 1976), especially for those age 75 and older (Kelly & Ross, 1989; Romsa, Bondy, & Blenman, 1983) because those personal interactions help contribute to social integration and reduce feelings of isolation in later life. Romsa et al. noted that activities reflecting belongingness and self-esteem have the greatest effect on quality of life. Interestingly, Mishra (1992) found that only social interaction with *non-family* members was associated with life satisfaction among retirees; similarly, Lemon et al. (1972) reported earlier that the only kind of informal social interaction associated with life satisfaction among in-movers to a retirement community was interaction with friends. In their replication of the Lemon et.al., study, however, Longino and Kart (1982) found that all types of informal social interaction, not just interaction with friends, were associated with life satisfaction among retirees. The activities of the gusto women were consistent with this latter finding, as illustrated by the woman who felt that the most enriching part of retirement was being able to spend more time with both family and friends. Another gusto woman focused on family when she described the importance of the grandmother role in her life: "The real gusto for me at this stage of my life is also evidenced through my role as grandma to two lovable, yet very active grandchildren. Being able to spend time with them and to get involved in various activities with them brings a great deal of pleasure to my life...."

A second very important area of activity in retirement is formal participation in community organizations and/or volunteer work. Moen, Fields, Quick, and Hofmeister (2000) observe that, as in the case of informal social interaction, participation in volunteer work and community organizations can substitute for paid employment and provide a means of social integration for retirees. In their Cornell Retirement and Well-Being Study, retirees who participated in multiple activities such as volunteering, clubs and other organizations, and even part-time work were found to have the highest levels of energy, mastery, and quality of life. Likewise, Mishra (1992) found that participation in voluntary organizations contributed to life satisfaction among retirees. Volunteering often provides meaning to the individual and is also socially valued; for those reasons it may be associated with well-being in later life (Morrow-Howell, 2010). All studies, however, do not support an association between formal social participation of some sort and psychological well-being; for example, Cutler and Danigelis (1993) reported that participation in religiously-related activities was the only formal activity that led to psychological well-being in their sample.

Most of the gusto women were involved in organizational activities and/or volunteering, many of them exhaustively, and they reported enjoying those activities enormously. One woman serves on the governing board of her sorority and on the board of trustees of a college, both of which involve extensive travel. Another woman is involved in fundraising and scholarships for Florida universities, was elected to the board of directors of the International Association of Retirement Associations in

Higher Education, and serves on the board of a non-profit multi-media company that provides education through the arts. A third woman has held several elected positions in a national organization for supervisors of mathematics education and chaired an Achievement Gap Task Force of the National Council of Teachers of Mathematics, both of which are related to her professional training and interests. In addition, she chairs the Commission on Christian Education at her church. Service on boards is likewise an important activity for a fourth woman, who serves on the board of a Florida hospital and also on the board of the Florida State University Medical School. The number of volunteer activities that the gusto women were asked to engage in could be somewhat overwhelming at times. Consequently, one woman established her own criteria for choosing activities that might serve as a guide to others in retirement: the activity should be a learning experience; it should help others; and it should be enjoyable and fun.

There is evidence that in addition to more organized kinds of activity, solitary activities such as reading, watching television, listening to music, and hobbies can be satisfying ways to spend one's time in retirement (Bevil et al, 1993; Peppers, 1976; Sener et al., 2007). This was the case for a number of the gusto women, one of whom had learned to play the cello and was spending time enjoying that instrument. Another woman was doing handwork that included making over one hundred origami boxes for colleagues in the School of Music on her campus. And a third woman, a retired physician, not only took up painting in retirement but serves as a "paper boy" by delivering papers to residents' doors in her retirement community when she takes her early morning walks; this both helps her to stay physically fit and provides a service to others.

Conclusion

The case studies in this book reveal a rather remarkable group of professional women, many of them are retired teachers, professors, and administrators, who remain very active during their retirement years, some until quite advanced ages. Most of the women appeared to have adequate health to be able to maintain a high activity level. The "gusto women" displayed a good deal of continuity in their activities, but some also took on new activities in retirement. Although some of the women confessed to being a bit "at sea" in the early years of retirement until they had developed a different and fulfilling lifestyle, all seemed to be ultimately satisfied with their retirement. As one put it: "It comes when you can say goodbye to the tension and hello to the pension." The women as a group were impressive in displaying high energy, commitment, interest in the world around them, and a desire to give back and help others. Some had "re-invented" themselves in new roles which gave life meaning. In the life stories that many of the women shared, it was not only retirement but the entire life course and the patterning of their lives and goals that were described. In this way, the women often revealed the basic values, such as lifetime commitment to a calling and a desire to help others and to give back to their communities, that had guided them earlier in their lives and that still do.

One caveat is that one cannot generalize women's retirement experience from these case studies of professional women to other groups of women, but only to that particular occupational group. Retirement may be a much different experience for women who are not as well educated and have fewer financial resources than do these women. For instance, some of the women spoke of extensive traveling in retirement, which many less economically fortunate women may not be able to afford. That said, however, the case studies and life stories provide a window into the lives of today's retired professional women, a group that will undoubtedly grow in size and make its influence felt in coming years. The lives of many of these "gusto women" are truly inspiring and can serve as a model of activity and social engagement for other women as they approach old age. It was a privilege and a pleasure to have the opportunity to have a window into their lives. (In the interest of full disclosure: I am myself a recent (2010) academic retiree).

References

Atchley, R.C. (1993).Continuity theory and the evolution of activity in later adulthood. In J. R. Kelly (Ed.), *Activity and aging* (pp. 5-16). Newbury Park, CA: Sage.

Atchley, R.C. (1999). *Continuity and adaptation in aging*. Baltimore, MD: John Hopkins University Press

Atchley, R. C. (2003). Why most people cope well with retirement. In J. R. Ronch & J. a. Goldfield (Eds.), *Mental wellness in aging:Strength-based approaches.* Baltimore, MD: Health Professions Press

Baltes, P. B., & Baltes, M.M. (1990). Selective optimization and compensation. In P. B.

Baltes & M.M. Baltes (Eds.), *Successful aging: Perspectives from the behavioral sciences* (pp. 1-34). New York: Cambridge University Press

Baltes, M.M. & Carstensen, L.L. (1996). The process of successful aging. *Aging and Society*, *16*,397-422.

Bevil, C.A., O'Connor, P.C., & Matton, P. M. (1993). Leisure activity, Life satisfaction, and perceived health status in older adults. *Gerontology and Geriatrics Education*, *14*, 3-19.

Cohen, G. (2003). The social portfolio: The role of activity in mental wellness as people age. In J. R. Ronch & J.A. Goldfield (Eds.), *Mental Wellness in aging: Strength-based approaches* (pp. 113-122). Baltimore, MD: Health Professions Press.

Cumming, E., & Henry, W.E. (1961). *Growing old: The process of disengagement.* New York: Basic Books.

Cutler, S. J., & Danigelis, N. L. (1993). Organized contexts of activity. In J. R. Kelly (Ed.), *Activity and aging* (pp. 146-163). Newbury Park, CA: Sage.

Elder, G. H., Jr. Johnson, M. K., & Crosnoe, R. (2003). The emergence and development of life course theory. In Mortimer, J., & Shanahan, J. (Eds.), *Handbook of the life course* (pp. 3-19). New York: Kluwer Academic/Plenum.

Floyd, F. J., Haynes, S. N., Doll, E. R. Winemiller, D., Lamsky, C.,Burgy, T.M., et. Al. (1992). Assessing retirement satisfaction and perceptions of retirement experiences. *Psychology and Aging, 7,* 609-621.

Freysinger, V., Alessio, H., & Mehdizadeh, S. (1993). Re-examining The morale-physical health-activity relationship: A longitudinal study of time changes and gender differences. *Activities, Adaptations, & Aging, 17,* 25-41.

Guinn, B. (1999). Leisure behavior motivation and the life satisfaction of retired persons. *Activities, Adaptation & Aging*, *23*, 13-20.

Havighurst, R.J., & Albrecht, R. (1953). *Older people.* New York:Longman, Green & Co.

Iwasaki, Y., & Smale, B. J. A. (1998). Longitudinal analyses of the relationships among life transitions, chronic health problems leisure and psychological well-being. *Leisure Sciences, 20,*20-52.

Kelly, J. R. (1982). Leisure in later life: Roles and identities. In N. J. Osgood (Ed.), *Life after work: Retirement, leisure, recreation and the elderly* (pp. 268-292). New York: Preager.

Kelly, J. R. & Ross, J. (1998). Later-life leisure: Beginning a new agenda. *Leisure Sciences 11,* 47-59.

Lemon, B. W., Bengston, V.L. & Peterson, J. A, (1972). An exploration of the activity theory of aging: Activity types and life satisfaction among in-movers to a retirement community. *Journal of Gerontology, 27*, 511-523.

Litwin, H., & Shiovitiz-Ezra, S. (2006). The association between activity and wellbeing in later life: What really matters? *Ageing & Society. 26*, 225-242.

Longino, C.F., & Kart, C. S. 1982). Explicating activity theory: a formal replication. *Journal of Gerontology, 37*, 713-722.

McGuire, F. A., Boyd, R. K., & Tedrick, R. E. (2009). *Leisure and aging* (4th ed.). Champaign, IL: Sagamore Publishing.

Menec, V. H. (2003). The relation between everyday activities and successful aging: A 6-year longitudinal study. *Journal of Gerontology: Social Sciences,* 58B, S74-S82.

Mishra, S. (1992). Leisure activities and life satisfaction in old age: A case study of re-tired government employees living in urban areas. *Activities, Adaptation & Aging, 16,* 7-26.

Moen, P. Fields, V., Quick, H. E., & Hofmeister, H. (2000). A life-course approach to retirement and social integration. In K. Pillemer, P., Moen, E. Wetherington, & N. Glasgow (Eds), *Social integration in the second half of life* (pp. 76-107). Baltimore, MD: Johns Hopkins University Press.

Morrow-Howell, N. (2010). Volunteering in later life: Research frontiers. *Journal of Gerontology: Social Sciences, 65B,*461-469.

Nimrod, G., & Kleiber, D. A. (2007). Reconsidering change and continuity in later life: Toward an innovation theory of successful aging. *International Journal of Aging and Human Development, 65*, 1-22.

O'Brien, G. E. (1981). Leisure attributes and retirement satisfaction. *Journal of Applied Psychology, 66*, 371-384.

Peppers, L. G. (1976). Patterns of leisure and adjustment to retirement. *The Gerontologist, 16*, 441-446.

Romsa, G., Bondy, P., & Blenman, M. (1985). Modeling retirees' life satisfaction levels: The role of recreational, life cycle, and socio-environmental elements. *Journal of Leisure Research,17*, 29-39.

Rowe, J. W., & Kahn, R. L. (1997) Successful aging. *The Gerontologist, 37*, 433-440.

Sener, A., Terzioglu, R. G. & Karabutlut, E. (2007). Life satisfaction and leisure activities during men's retirement: A Turkish sample. Aging & *Mental Health, 11*, 30-36.

Biographies of Authors

Barbara Barnes, Ph.D., former Provost and Professor, College of Education, Florida A and M University. Her doctoral studies were completed at Florida State University.

Marie E. Cowart, Dr.P.H., Currently Dean and Professor Emerita, Formerly Professor of Urban and Regional Planning and Dean, College of Social Sciences, Florida State University, Her Degrees are from the University of Florida, Tulane University, and Columbia University.

Joel Dawson, Ph.D., Retired Public School Administrator who served as an elementary school Principal, an alternative high school Principal, and the district's Science Coordinator. She holds membership in numerous organizations including Zonta Club of Tallahassee and is an award winning photographer. She received her Ph.D. in Science Education from Florida State University.

Lorraine Dorfman, Ph. D., Professor, School of Social Work and Aging Studies Program, University of Iowa. She received her Ph.D. from the University of Iowa.

Clinita Arnsby Ford, Ph.D., Professor Emeritus, Florida A and M University, Director National Higher Education Conferences on Minority Student Education.

Linda Fulmore, Ph.D., Currently, Education Mathematics and Equity Consultant. Formerly teacher of high school mathematics, Phoenix, Arizona. Her Ph.D. is from Northern Arizona University.

Fanchon F. Funk, Ed.D., Professor Emerita, College of Education Department of Educational Leadership and Policy Studies, Florida State; Director Alumni Affairs, College of Education Dean's Office at Florida State University. Her Ed.D is from The University of Tennessee, Knoxville.

Freddie Groomes-Mclendon, Ph.D., Former Executive Assistant to the President of Florida State University and Professor of Education. Her Ph.D. is from Florida State University.

Mrs. Alyce Goff, M.S., Music educator, arranger, and performer. She received her MS in Education from Baylor University.

Mrs. Lucy Ho, Currently owner of two restaurants in Tallahassee Florida, Director of Costume Design for FSU School of Music Opera Program. She received her education at the Trebien Dressmaking School in Taipei and at the Indiana University History of Costume and Costume Design Program.

Ruth Hobbs, Ph.D., Former Executive/Divisional Director, Department of Intervention and Community Services, Leon County Schools, Tallahassee, Florida. Her doctorate is from Florida A and M University.

Charlotte Maguire, M.D., Retired Private Pediatric Practice in Orlando Florida, and the Florida Department of Health and Rehabilitative Services. Her education was received at the College of Medicine, University of Arkansas.

Jill Quadagno, Ph.D., Mildred and Claude Pepper Eminent Scholar in Social Gerontology and Professor Sociology, Florida State University. Her Ph.D. is from the University of Kansas. She is Past President, American Sociological Association.

Penny Ralston, Ph.D., Professor, College of Human Sciences and Director, Center Better Health and Life for Underserved Populations, Florida State University. Former Dean College of Human Sciences, Florida State University. Her Ph.D. is from the University of Illinois at Champaign-Urbana.

Mrs. Marjorie Reitz Turnbull, former State Legislator and Leon County Commissioner; former Vice President for Institutional Advancement and Executive Director of the Foundation at Tallahassee Community College. Her undergraduate degree is from the University of Florida and she holds the MA in Political Science from the University of Georgia.

Freddie Groomes-McLendon
Editor

Early in her career as an educator in Gadsden County, Florida, Groomes-McLendon was among the first teachers hired at new Northside High School, in Havana. It was there that she began to experience gusto in her career. She initiated the first high school class in Home economics for boys in the county. It proved to be quite popular to the surprise of naysayers who said that young men would not take the course.

While at Florida A & M University she wrote a proposal and was funded in excess of one million dollars by the US Department of Education for a project to establish the first Consortium for Institutional Research at Historical Black Colleges and Universities.

In 1972 it was no surprise when J. Stanley Marshall, President of Florida State University hired her as the first African-American and first woman to serve in the university's central administration as a member of the University Council that provided administrative leadership for the University. It was under her leadership that the University became prominent in the area of Affirmative action and the recruitment and graduation of African-American students.

Upon her retirement Groomes-McLendon continued to write and address the concerns of young and seasoned professionals. She authored a book "The Marginal Difference" that is used by aspiring professionals as well and high school and college students.

More recently she was motivated to invite twelve of her retired friends and colleagues to join her in the development of a very unique book "Real Gusto Comes Later: How Professional Women Experience Retirement."

This diverse group of women who have had very successful careers are now experiencing Real Gusto in life as they reinvent themselves and take on expanded or new experiences utilizing in many cases their earlier professional expertise.

www.ingramcontent.com/pod-product-compliance
Lightning Source LLC
Chambersburg PA
CBHW072143270326
41931CB00010B/1871